"*Human-Centered Agile* incorporates Human-Centered Design thinking and tools into the agile practice environment. The book offers practical ways to combine these two disciplines and scale as needed. In this book you can expect to learn:

- A process for Human-Centered Design activities and artifacts alignment with Agile practices that will build better products.
- How product lifecycle work such as evaluating stakes, defining a problem statement and evaluating products in the hands of users can be seamlessly integrated with the Agile workflow.
- How Research Roadmaps can run parallel to the product roadmap and provide a clear picture of the overall workload.
- The elements of research stories and sample stories with acceptance criteria.
- Tips on how to scale Human-Centered Agile from one team to many teams.
- How Human-Centered Design continuous evaluation aligns with continuous deployments.
- How Research Roadmaps scale and work with the Architectural Runway.
- Ideas for creating an Insight Repository and lessons learned from incorporating these frameworks into one seamless methodology.

This comprehensive guide helps you determine how much and when from the discovery and ideation phase to evaluating the end-product in the customer's hands!"

Diane Brady
Enterprise Agile Coach
Co-author of *The Agile Almanac Book Two: Programs with Multi- and Virtual-Team Environments*

"Human-Centered Agile introduces a much-needed topic with practical advice on how to apply the concept and approach from the smallest agile team to the largest product portfolio. The approach addresses many anti-patterns that can happen with well-intentioned agile teams. The book has the best practical advice I have encountered to address a frequent struggle as agile scales - How do you maintain continuity with the user's experience as development is scaled out across multiple agile teams? Joe and Brad have done the heavy lifting for the rest of us and have figured out how to map the concept of Human-Centered Design to whatever flavor of agile development you might be doing."

Douglas Peyton Martin
Author of *Project Management Hacking*

"Ready to give your organization the competitive edge it needs? Look no further than *Human-Centered Agile* by Montalbano & Lehman. This groundbreaking book is the ultimate guide for Change Leaders seeking to revolutionize their approach to Agile and enterprise transformation. Packed with real-world examples and actionable strategies, this must-read resource will empower you to not only deliver effectively but also accelerate innovation throughout your entire organization. Whether you're an executive or organizational coach, this book is essential for anyone looking to stay ahead in today's fast-paced business environment."

Jorgen Hesselberg
Author of *Unlocking Agility: An Insider's Guide
to Agile Enterprise Transformation*
Co-founder of Comparative Agility

"Human-Centered Agile is a holistic approach to integrating Agile and Human-Centered Design (HCD) that facilitates vital enterprise-agility, the focus of my work for the past decade. Agile and HCD both operate concurrently and interactively, energizing and focusing on the product delivery lifecycle, which is the determinant of future organizational success. Conceptually, Human-Centered Agile is simply teams doing both things at the same time, unleashing amazing results consistently.

Human-Centered Agile (HCA) is a *must have* competitive necessity for delivering a powerful *organizational impact*. It is a new way of working and thinking that creates a successful competitive response to an ever more insane marketplace, making mastery of product and delivery an existential determinant. Thus, HCA should not be treated as an HCD "bolt-on" accessory for the Agile process.

The existential reality of today's marketplace competition means only organizations that quickly deliver the "correct" solution will survive, much less thrive. That requires building "something" and obtaining user feedback, which Agile methods provide. The genius of Human-Centered Agile is that it provides a toolkit to improve that "something" from the very first iteration! Human-Centered Agile simultaneously and continuously accelerates the integration of learning into product development, thereby delivering better products faster and, ultimately, unleashing enterprise-wide agility . . . and the ability to thrive!"

John G. Stenbeck, PMP, CDAI, CSP,
Three-time Amazon #1 Best Selling Author, *Enterprise Agility Expert*

Human-Centered Agile

This book is a guide on how to apply Human-Centered Design (HCD) practices to an Agile product development model that is used widely throughout industry and government, where it is applied primarily to software and technology development efforts. This has been an ongoing industry challenge due to the fact that HCD prioritizes time spent understanding the problems to be solved (time spent in the problem space), while Agile prioritizes a fast hypothesize-and-deliver model (time spent in the solution space).

Organizations that attempt an Agile transformation abandon it either because it was too difficult or because it did not deliver the hoped-for results. At the same time, efforts to improve the design and experience of their products using HCD have a tendency to fall short because it can be difficult to see the ROI of design efforts, even while companies like McKinsey document design-driven successes. What's more, a company that successfully adopts Agile often seems to have an even harder time implementing HCD and vice versa. This is particularly disappointing since Agile and HCD should be mutually supportive.

In practice, Agile teams often bypass HCD efforts in favor of finishing their goals and thinking they are doing well, only to have their work product fail to meet the actual end user's needs. At first the team will become indignant. "We followed the expert guidance of our Product Owner, the 'Voice of the Customer,'" they will say, followed by "but . . . it met all of the Acceptance Criteria, they should love it." It's a failure of Agile that this type of suboptimal delivery happens so regularly and predictably. The fact that team responses can be so accurately predicted in advance (by those who've seen this movie many times before) points to a process failure or inefficiency that is widespread and desperately needs to be addressed.

Alternatively, teams will invest too heavily in up-front discovery efforts that slow down delivery to an unacceptable point, often while also failing to capture research-based findings in a way that matures the overall strategic product or portfolio understanding. The cost of misfiring goes far beyond a bad delivery or an angry customer. Decreased team morale drives poorer future performance (cost), turnover if left unchecked (more cost), and nonproductive blame sessions that lead to degraded faith in the Agile product development model itself.

This book identifies solutions based on successful methods of integrating HCD practices by phase into an ongoing agile delivery model, from discovery through implementation and evaluation, including:

- key success factors for an HCD/Agile engagement approach,
- critical points of delivery, and
- strategies for integrating HCD into teams based on the existing design maturity of an organization or product team.

Human-Centered Agile
A Unified Approach for Better Outcomes

Joe Montalbano | Brad Lehman
Developmental Editor: Lauren Mix
Illustrations: Sandra Dorr
Cover art: Ed Galm

Foreword by Luke Hohmann

Routledge
Taylor & Francis Group

A PRODUCTIVITY PRESS BOOK

First published 2024
by Routledge
605 Third Avenue, New York, NY 10158

and by Routledge
4 Park Square, Milton Park, Abingdon, Oxon, OX14 4RN

Routledge is an imprint of the Taylor & Francis Group, an informa business

ISBN: 978-1-032-03690-8 (hbk)
ISBN: 978-1-032-03689-2 (pbk)
ISBN: 978-1-003-18852-0 (ebk)

DOI: 10.4324/9781003188520

Typeset in Garamond
by Apex CoVantage, LLC

For my wife, Julie, for always knowing the right thing to say . . .
and when to just listen. And for my sister, Kathy,
and her husband, Bill, two of the best people
(and parents and grandparents!) I've ever known.

Joe Montalbano

For Lorelei, who got me into this whole mess to begin with,
for which I am forever grateful. I could not have had a better
first UX mentor. And for Fox, who seems to think that I know
way more than I do about life. For now, at least.

Brad Lehman

Contents

Figures

Foreword

Pundits assert that the technology is changing "faster than ever" and that we need to keep pace.

Sure. But how?

One approach is to embrace innovations that help us develop software quickly and efficiently. Such things as DevOps, automation, and AI-enhanced development environments are among the many examples of innovations that help us serve customers better.

Another is to develop an understanding and appreciation of timeless principles and embrace them.

This is where the integration of Human-Centered Design, agile software development, and the scaled agile framework comes into play. These methodologies, when combined, create a powerful approach to software development that puts the customer at the center of the development process, while also promoting collaboration, flexibility, and continuous improvement.

In this book, Joe and Brad have taken on the challenging task of integrating these methodologies into a cohesive approach to user-centric software development. They have drawn on their extensive experience in the field to provide practical guidance on how to use Human-Centered Design to identify and understand customer needs, how to implement agile software development practices to quickly and iteratively develop software, and how to use the Scaled Agile Framework to effectively manage large-scale software development projects.

One of the things that I appreciate about this book is the way that it takes a holistic approach to software development. It recognizes that developing software is not just about writing code, but also about understanding the needs of customers and ensuring that the software meets those needs. It also recognizes that software development is a team sport, and that effective collaboration and communication are essential for success.

Whether you are a software developer, project manager, or business leader, this book provides valuable insights and guidance on how to use Human-Centered Design, agile software development, and the scaled agile framework to develop software that meets the needs of your customers while also delivering value to your organization. I highly recommend it to anyone who is interested in improving their software development practices.

Luke Hohmann

Author of *Innovation Games* and *Beyond Software Architecture*

co-Author of *Software Profit Streams*™

SAFe Contributor

Chief Innovation Officer, Applied Frameworks

Preface

The techniques described in this book were pioneered at a large government agency that we cannot name. Management had been using Agile methods for years and knew that Agile allowed them to learn faster and deliver faster with more predictability and higher quality. They also had success using Human-Centered Design (HCD) methods to get better insight into the needs, attitudes, and priorities of their customers and end users. Unfortunately, their Agile and HCD initiatives were siloed and divorced from one another.

Their request seemed simple enough: Get the experts who had successfully led their transition to Agile methods to collaborate with experts in HCD to give them a "best of both worlds" implementation. Of course! It was common sense. It sounded easy.

The reality was that combining these ways of thinking and working turned out to be much harder than anyone expected it to be. Agile practitioners initially misunderstood the need for HCD. "Can't we just iterate our solution and refine it with feedback until we get it right?" HCD practitioners, however, were often included as an afterthought in the early stages, leading to less-than-optimal outcomes and not just a little bit of frustration and hurt feelings.

One day we were having lunch and brainstorming through some implementation challenges, and we joked that "we should write a book about this." As the engagement went on and we had our fair share of hard-fought victories as well as stinging defeats, the idea of documenting our experiences and sharing them with the Agile and HCD communities kept coming up more and more frequently. Every time we learned something the quip was "that's another chapter."

At some point, our client finally got to their desired state with "Human-Centered Agile." We wrote a SAFe® Advanced Topics article about our experiences and then presented a talk about our experiences at the Agile 2021 Conference (which was virtual due to COVID-19). It seemed like we had not only a set of lessons learned but also some successes and client outcomes to go with them, and we started writing in earnest.

This book is the result of those lessons learned and is designed to help Agilists and HCD practitioners build "best of breed" programs of their own while avoiding all the mistakes we made. We hope that the ideas and techniques presented here can help make existing Agile programs even better and help HCD practitioners iterate more predictably with better outcomes for both.

Acknowledgments

We would like to acknowledge and thank the following people and organizations for their help and guidance during the preparation of this manuscript:

Lorelei Brown and Dawn Barton for their time and wisdom.

Sandy Dorr for her awesome illustrations and good humor through ceaseless rounds of changes. And more changes.

Ed Galm for his cover art.

Lauren Mix for her developmental editorial prowess.

Our friends at Scaled Agile, Inc: Dr. Steve Mayner, Marc Rix, Kevin Wells, Stosh Misiaszek, David Freed, Michelle Stoll, Lorienne Neska, and Risa Wilmeth for their help with copyright permissions, article review, graphics, and such.

Jen Cardello whose formulation of "right problem, right solution, done right" has heavily influenced our approach.

Luke Hohmann for generously donating his time, his sage guidance, and for the gift of feedback.

John Stenbeck for his mentorship, advice, and wisdom.

Mike Torppey and Bernardo Gonzales; without their vision and perseverance the first Human-Centered Agile project wouldn't have happened.

Our advance readers for their time, attention, and fantastic feedback. This book would have been very different without all of you: Ann Aly, Sree Bhandaram, Michael Brown, Catherine Cartwright, Bella Jones, Anneliese LaTempa, Doug Martin, Diane McCann, Paul McInerny, Jeff Nichols, Amelia Shuler, James Sperry, David Tilghman, and Michael Williams.

About the Authors

Joe Montalbano is a Management Consultant, Enterprise Agile Coach, and business Agility expert with over 20 years' experience, primarily in large software development environments. He has successfully led multiple, large-scale Agile transitions and managed dozens of software development efforts using numerous onshore, offshore, distributed, and virtual development teams. He also has hands-on skills throughout the Microsoft technology stack.

Joe is an enthusiastic coach, teacher, and facilitator. He holds certifications including CSP, SPC, KMP, PMI-ACP, PMP, and is a SAFe Contributor. He is co-author of the Amazon #1 best-selling book *Agile Almanac Book 2: Programs with Multi- and Virtual Team Environments* and has an MBA from Johns Hopkins University. He is an avid wildlife photographer and a less avid amateur radio operator. This is his second book.

Brad Lehman began as a front-end coder when his girlfriend (now wife) taught him HTML so that he could create a website for his record label ("Best viewed in Netscape 3.0 or better!"). He became a "design team of one" shortly after that and has been working with Agile teams and programs since 2010. He is also a husband, parent, design coach, community radio DJ, and avid coffee roaster and drinker.

Introduction—How This Book is Organized

The goal of this book is to help readers integrate Human-Centered Design (HCD) practices into Agile in a way that extends the Agile mindset and supports teams in their work and that lets them learn and deliver truly valuable products faster and at lower risk. We've divided the content into six parts so that you can easily find the content most valuable to you.

Part I—Introducing Human-Centered Agile

Chapter 1—What Is Human-Centered Agile, and Why Is It Needed?

This is an introduction to what Human-Centered Agile is and why we think it is important. Part I articulates the foundation of what Human-Centered Agile is and starts to get readers thinking in the "Human-Centered Agile" mindset. This chapter also explores why it is such a challenge for HCD and Agile to work together and proposes a framework for aligning the two mindsets.

Part II—Understanding Just Enough HCD

Chapter 2—A Primer on Human-Centered Design
Chapter 3—HCD Activities and Artifacts from Discovery through Concept Validation
Chapter 4—HCD Activities and Artifacts from Refinement through Evaluation

This part is an introduction to HCD for those who need it. It introduces phases of the design process and goes a little deeper into both the activities and artifacts that comprise HCD work in each of these phases. This section gives the reader both a *what* and a *why* of the HCD activities and artifacts that should be brought into their Agile program.

Part III—How Much and When? Planning and Executing HCD Within Agile

This part seeks to dispel the misguided myths that HCD "needs to slow you down" and that "we are trying to see around every corner" (or "boil the ocean"; pick your preferred metaphor). Human-Centered Agile doesn't prescribe that every research step needs to happen for every effort. Instead, Human-Centered Agile aligns the research effort to the expected impact and risk of a solution being delivered, with specific learning goals at each step. These chapters describe how to do that.

Part IV—Larger Programs, Different Needs

As programs grow in both size and stakes, their research and design need to grow as well. This growth means coordination and operations at a program level, not just a team level. This part is useful for readers who are at this awkward stage of growth on their own programs, and it also lays the groundwork for the next section on scaling Human-Centered Agile.

Part V—The Largest Programs: Human-Centered Agile and SAFe®

Chapter 14—Delivery at Scale: The SAFe® Continuous Delivery Pipeline

This section focuses on how to apply Human-Centered Agile at scale on programs with hundreds or even thousands of people working on them, which introduces additional challenges. This section uses SAFe® as a reference point to discuss how to practice Human-Centered Agile at scale. Don't worry, this section also provides an orientation for practitioners who have never worked with SAFe before.

Part VI—Measuring and Applying Human-Centered Agile

Chapter 15—Measuring Solution Performance
Chapter 16—Human-Centered Agile Applied

The final part begins with a discussion about how Product Owners and Product Managers might measure solution performance and why such measurement is critical to Human-Centered Agile. The part closes with a case study in which Human-Centered Agile is applied at a fictitious company.

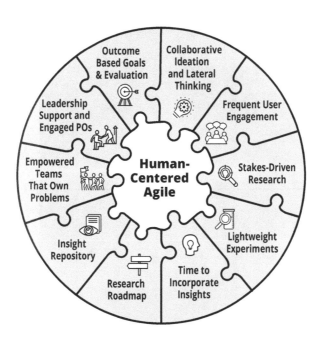

Figure 0.1   Key themes in *Human-Centered Agile*.

Note: PO = Product Owner.

It is our hope that this final section illustrates the core themes of Human-Centered Agile (see Figure 0.1) and ties them together in a way that helps readers synthesize and apply them to their own programs.

There are several core themes that show up throughout the book. A quick reference on finding them in the text:

- Collaborative ideation and lateral thinking (Chapter 2)
- Frequent user engagement (Chapter 3)
- Lightweight experiments (Chapter 5)
- Stakes-driven research (Chapter 6)
- Time to incorporate insights (Chapter 7)
- A Research Roadmap (Chapter 7)
- An insight repository (Chapter 9)
- Empowered teams that own problems (Chapter 10)
- Leadership support and engaged Product Owners and Product Managers (Chapter 10)

INTRODUCING HUMAN-CENTERED AGILE

Chapter 1

What Is Human-Centered Agile, and Why Is It Needed?

Agile and Human-Centered Design (HCD) are two widely used disciplines that strive for similar outcomes but often struggle to "speak" to one another. HCD and Agile have embraced ways of working that focus on different phases of a delivery process. While they share some similar goals of learning about what product users want so that they can deliver useful solutions, the two disciplines have very different mindsets. Because of this, when asked to apply both disciplines, Agile and HCD practitioners struggle to understand each other's point of view and often craft a process that lacks the necessary time in both the problem and solution spaces. When Agile and HCD practitioners work together, they are often unable to explain to business stakeholders what should happen and when.

This can take the form of direct competition, or even conflict, as Agile-driven teams see HCD as either an obstacle or direct competitor for resources, while HCD practitioners struggle to gain ground with the early-phase efforts that can be very valuable in the long run. Attempting to integrate the HCD competency into an existing Agile program often results in friction, inefficiency, and conflict.

It doesn't have to be this way. This book proposes a way for these two disciplines to get along and deliver better outcomes.

Human-Centered Agile is a holistic, simultaneous application of Agile product development and HCD throughout the product life cycle. This helps teams generate insights, validate designs, and get a faster evaluation

DOI: 10.4324/9781003188520-2

of both designs and finished work than either Agile or HCD could by themselves. Human-Centered Agile is not the mere inclusion of HCD as a "bolt-on" to the Agile process but rather a whole new way of working and thinking that is integrated into Agile delivery from beginning to end. To achieve Human-Centered Agile, there isn't one single place in the Agile workflow where HCD is applied.

Human-Centered Agile uses user insights gathered through HCD methods to better inform every event and artifact throughout the Agile life cycle. Human-Centered Agile provides the ability for a single team to apply HCD methods to test a hypothesis, discover user needs, or even figure out which approaches don't work. This feels different from traditional Agile (see Figure 1.1). The customer is more present and involved, removing the Product Owner from standing between the team and end users. Users are consulted directly and continuously through development and even after deployment. This activity is planned and baked into the process.

The Human-Centered Agile team is given permission to think about what needs to be built before building something, compare several design options, and mitigate risk by validating their assumptions through activities that generate user understanding. This stands in contrast to picking a Minimum Viable Product (MVP) and building it and only *then* getting user feedback.

Incorporating HCD thinking and tools into Agile teams helps them deliver the most value to the user. Three basic yet crucial questions that teams should be asking throughout the product life cycle are:

- "Are we solving the right problem?" (***right problem***)
- "Is this the best solution, given all of our constraints?" (***right solution***)
- "Are we delivering this solution correctly?" (***done right***)

Answering these questions is essential to delivering products in a cost-effective way. While traditional Agile frequently takes a "build it and see" approach to answering all three questions at once (sometimes after a good deal of work has been put in), HCD practitioners seek to learn the answers to these questions in earlier stages. To effectively do this in an Agile framework, HCD practitioners integrate a variety of tools and methodologies across the Agile workflow.

Key elements of Human-Centered Agile are:

- The use of HCD methods throughout the entire Agile process can address traditional gaps in Agile, specifically around ***discovery***, ***ideation***, and ***concept validation***. This gives teams tools to enhance the Product Owner's understanding of users' needs.
- Human-Centered Agile is a holistic process whereby one team focuses on a problem and is responsible for the outcome.
- HCD practices are applied proportionately with the "***stakes***" or risk of a product or enhancement in Human-Centered Agile. The greater the stakes, the more investment teams will make in generating—and acting on—insights from real users.
- Human-Centered Agile gives teams the tools and permission they need to plan HCD work that might not be consumed during the current sprint, something that might not feel Agile at first but that is a major success factor for Human-Centered Agile teams. Human-Centered Agile allows for teams to plan and execute HCD work that intentionally won't be consumed immediately. This is done using a "***Research Roadmap***" to align HCD activities with development and delivery activities.
- The ability to scale as the number of teams grows. Gaps in discovery, ideation, and concept validation get worse with scale. Methods used in Human-Centered Agile work just as well at scale as they do on a small stand-alone team.
- Human-Centered Agile brings HCD findings into product strategy. Strategy is constantly informed—and updated—based on fresh insight from users and teams.

WHAT IS INSIGHT?

The outcomes of an HCD research activity are commonly referred to as "insights," regardless of the activity type or specific methodology being used. An ***insight*** is a fancy way of expressing an understanding of a user's attitude, behavior, or expectation, which helps teams build products that will successfully match those expectations and behaviors while learning what will improve their experience. HCD practitioners interview users, collect sentiment from message boards and support tickets, or conduct usability tests to gather insights, which then get captured in any number of deliverables, ranging from **personas** (archetypes of users that have common goals and characteristics) and **scenarios** or **journey maps** (descriptions of a specific process or series of connected user activities, informed by user sentiment). These are collected and documented (possibly in an insight repository) in order to create a durable place where a Product Owner or manager can review what has been gathered across multiple research efforts.

Agile and HCD as Practiced Separately

Over the past decade or so, Agile has become the preferred method for software delivery because it allows for short release cycles that yield fast learning. As such, Agile replaced the previously used "Big Design Up Front" approach to refining requirements and delivering projects.

Agile has been a revolution in software delivery but has also produced some product design drawbacks. Time for the early-stage activities that help teams understand their users (called discovery) is often all but eliminated. The exploration of competing solution ideas (called ideation) is expected to happen in a very compressed timeframe, sometimes within the same sprint as development itself, if it happens at all. Evaluation work is often put off until after software is released, creating risks to the success of the product itself. Agile teams often spend most of their time thinking about the *execution* of solutions in an effort to deliver as quickly as possible. Thus, they mostly live in the "solution space."

At the same time—and perhaps because of these specific drawbacks—HCD, which can be thought of as a specific form of "**design thinking**," has gained popularity as a way to set a clear vision for products to be released that prioritizes understanding user needs from the very first steps. HCD develops solutions to problems by involving the human perspective in all steps of the problem-solving process. It ensures that products are delivered in such a way that they are more likely to be valuable to users upon release, not just after multiple rounds of refinement. In this way, much of HCD is spent thinking about the "**problem space**."

This dichotomy of Agile working in the **solution space**, and HCD working in the problem space is a general pattern, not an absolute divide. Agile teams write user stories from a user value perspective, and they learn from users through sequential releases. HCD incorporates the work of seeking feedback from users at each important step, iteratively, in the decision-making process about what that product will be. But, as a mindset, it's fair to say that Agile and HCD practitioners are often thinking in somewhat different terms.

Why Is Human-Centered Agile Needed?

> *In theory, theory and practice are the same. In practice, they are not.*
>
> **—attributed to Albert Einstein**

If it were easy to apply Agile and HCD practices at the same time, there would be no need for this book. It would all just happen. After all, they share a goal of delivering a better product to users faster and cheaper, which should make them naturally compatible.

Combining these two practices requires bridging the gap between different mindsets as well as trying to provide time and space for their specific activities. There are often different expectations about timeframes, planning horizons, what counts as key activities, and how and when decisions are best made. What's more, the challenges of integrating these two practices vary based on the size of the teams or programs running them. Product complexity and team size impact the required approach to integrating the two.

As Agile and HCD attempt to mingle, a resentful mentality may also develop. Established Agile-driven teams might view HCD as an obstacle to or a direct competitor of necessary resources, making HCD practitioners feel that they must justify their existence as they focus on the early-phase efforts that ultimately prove to be very valuable in the long run. HCD teams may feel shortchanged when asked to make decisions with little evidence or time.

It doesn't have to be this way.

Problem Space vs Solution Space

> *A problem well-stated is half-solved.*
>
> **—Charles Kettering**

Unraveling the difference in approach between Agile and HCD practitioners starts with an understanding of the difference between the problem

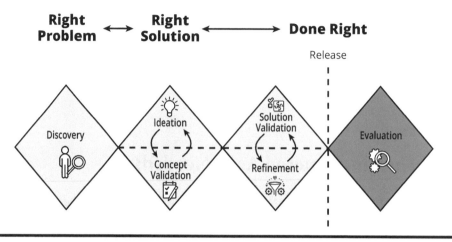

Figure 1.1   Right problem, right solution, done right.

space and the solution spaces. This distinction is the crux of much of the practical decision-making about how to build new products cheaply and effectively.

The problem space is where teams devote the time and attention needed to understand the problem they are trying to solve. This is the entire context of the solution, including an understanding of users and what they might need, team capabilities, business constraints, expected outcomes, and measures of success in relation to both those users and the business.

By contrast, the solution space is where teams devote the time and attention to solving any problem they have defined, making all the decisions about what a feature will be and how it will be delivered (see Figure 1.1). This includes ideation, user story writing, and the analysis of acceptance criteria (AC) or requirements that will be delivered, as well as sizing, prioritization, and execution of development work.

In thinking about the problem space versus the solution space, it is useful to ensure that teams are continuously asking the following three questions, best articulated by Jen Cardello, head of UX research and insights at Fidelity Investments:

- "Are we solving the right problem?" (right problem)
- "Is this the best solution, given all of our constraints?" (right solution)
- "Are we delivering this solution correctly?" (done right)

These questions are instrumental throughout the Human-Centered Agile life cycle. It is important to understand that, at any point, it is possible to learn new information that requires a team to revisit its original answers to *any* of these questions.

Right Problem

All of a team's work should solve an existing problem or need for the customer using the tool. A key principle from the Agile Manifesto states "Simplicity—the art of maximizing the amount of work not done—is essential."[1] The easiest, farthest upstream place to maximize work not done is by eliminating work that does not solve a genuine need.

Human-Centered Agile recognizes the value of understanding and clearly defining the problem to be solved—spending time in the problem space, to create a ***problem definition*** that gives the team a strong foundation. That problem definition needs to include user and business goals as well as a clear way to measure whether the team is creating successful **outcomes**, not just delivering features.

Right Solution

There are a variety of ways to solve any problem. Solution ideas can vary wildly in feasibility, cost, time to release, and value to the user. As Human-Centered Agilists, the goal is to identify the best solution that aligns the users' needs with the business goals of the product being delivered. Some problems can be solved with small-scale solutions, while others require larger efforts. Sometimes, the best that can be done is *to mitigate* a problem. Teams often find a strategy that blends short-term mitigation/improvement strategies with a long-term vision for a better experience.

It is important to determine that a solution is the right solution and that a solution be sustainable. Obviously, business and technical factors are critical inputs in this process. So, too, is considering whether a solution satisfies the users' needs and aligns with their goals and expectations. Without regard for users, teams run a real risk of developing products that look great to Product Owners on a whiteboard but fall flat on release.

---

[1] https://agilemanifesto.org/principles.html

Done Right

Perhaps the HCD work that is easiest to understand and most commonly incorporated within the development process belongs to the Done Right step, which validates the specific details of the product directly with users. Teams might do some usability testing to answer questions like Can they use the product without confusion? and Does it deliver on their expectations, both overall and at each step? There are any number of ways to elicit direct feedback, such as usability testing, targeted piloting and A/B (or multivariate) tests, and surveys.

Agile and HCD Practitioners Within Problem and Solution Space

Agile teams are used to working in the solution space with a Product Owner, who acts as the representative for customer needs and attitudes as well as the "value maximizer" on the team. It is the Product Owner's job to make decisions about what provides the most end-user value and ensure that the team always works on that.

Agile succeeds because teams build small increments of value as fast as they can. Then, upon receipt of user feedback, they iterate that solution until the Product Owner switches their focus to something else providing higher value. Ideally, this process is both ***incremental*** and ***iterative***, allowing teams to learn together as they deliver higher levels of value in small increments. There is also constant communication between the Agile team and the Product Owner throughout to improve the current and future processes.

It is important to understand that many Agile teams use the Product Owner as a proxy for the end user and have little or no interaction with *actual* end users. This creates the risk of delivering work that does not provide value should the Product Owner make a wrong decision or misinterpret the users' needs. This is a huge blind spot in Agile product development that Human-Centered Agile seeks to address.

By contrast, HCD practitioners are used to operating in the problem space and depend on interaction with end users. Like Agile teams, they seek knowledge about the needs of end users and information about how to craft a desirable solution to address those needs.

To achieve this, HCD practitioners have a variety of tools to help identify, refine, and catalog the needs and desires of end users before an MVP is ever built and evaluated after release. Instead of relying exclusively on the perspective of a Product Owner, HCD teams use direct interaction with end users to gain the knowledge earlier in the process that Agile teams gain through the creation of an MVP. They carry that knowledge into the solution space, where they generate visual representations of the solution to demonstrate and validate their understanding, evaluating the solution throughout the build and launch processes.

In reality, the divide between the problem space and solution space is not absolute. Even from the earliest points of discovery, stakeholders (including users) will propose specific solutions, and it is natural to think about how to solve a problem from the moment it is identified. Similarly, as solutions are developed and accepted or rejected by users, the nature of the problem being solved may get clearer and evolve. Teams should check in on both the problem and the solution throughout the ***delivery cycle***, understanding that the proportion of time and work spent in each space will change. At the beginning of the delivery cycle for a given product or feature, almost all of a team's focus should be on problem definition. Toward release, almost all the work is on delivering the solution.

UNDERSTANDING JUST ENOUGH HUMAN-CENTERED DESIGN

Chapter 2

A Primer on Human-Centered Design

Design is a tricky term—ask ten people what design means, and there will be twelve different answers. To understand Human-Centered Design (HCD), it's helpful to understand what is meant by design in this book.

Design is the intentional creation of a specific experience or outcome.

That's it. It doesn't matter whether the product being developed is a website or a chair (and boy, do Designers love their chairs!). An experience is created for the user of the product. When design is discussed, especially in software, people most often think about ***visual design***—the color palette, pictures, and balance of elements. Visual design is only one aspect, however. Additional aspects, such as ***interaction design***, information architecture, and ***content strategy***, are also vital to good software development, as are the research and testing activities that have become synonymous with "designing a user experience."

A common misunderstanding is that design is the *definition* of a specific experience or outcome in the same way that the blueprints and plans for a building are considered "the design." The *construction* of the building is also part of the design process. This includes each of the individual decisions that get made along the way (right down to the door handles!) that impact the way someone *experiences* the building, even if those decisions were made or changed after the initial plans were generated.

DOI: 10.4324/9781003188520-4

An artificial separation of design from delivery permeates the way teams think about design in software, too. The definition and planning of a product is completely separated from delivery. In practice, especially in software, this separation is rarely clear. Even after requirements are generated for a product, there will be decisions made during the delivery process that affect the end experience.

Gaps in the initial stories, technological constraints not fully understood initially, or unforeseen updates to business logic are all factors that can change the plan, and whoever is making these changes—Designer, Business Analyst, Developer, Product Owner—is, in that moment, *designing* the product. If teams fully separate the product *definition* from product *delivery*, they are ignoring the fact that the design is still happening throughout the process.

HCD = Research + Design

One of the evergreen pitfalls of design, especially HCD, is that the word *design* itself is prone to many misunderstandings. People often think of visual design and use terms like "look and feel," treating it as a coat of paint that follows all the team's important decisions. For this reason, terms like **UX**, **UI,** and *HCD* are used in an effort to distinguish what is meant. However, these terms have become buzzwords as much as they have become repositories for many different meanings, which makes vocabulary around design frustratingly slippery.

To be as clear as possible: **HCD is a combination of research and design.** Without research, there is no "human" in HCD. HCD is a methodology that aligns business goals with user needs from the outset of the design process by keeping the user (the human) in the frame throughout the product development lifecycle.

Introducing the Phases of HCD

HCD contains seven key steps: discovery, ideation, concept validation, refinement, solution validation, development, and evaluation (see Figure 2.1). This is true whether the design is simple or complex. The breadth and duration of these steps can vary greatly depending on the team's approach to delivering their product and their learning needs along the way.

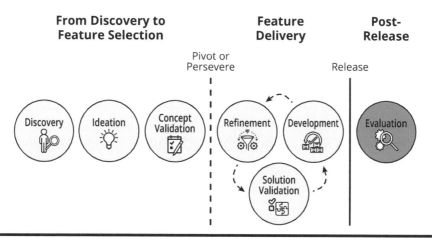

Figure 2.1 Phases of Human-Centered Design.

Discovery

Discovery generates the required input for the ideation effort, or the "right problem." The point of discovery is to define and articulate the problem to be solved, understand the context in which the solution can succeed (including the needs and attitudes of users), and properly assess the constraints on the range of possible solutions.

It is typical to see some of the following during the discovery process:

- Business-requirements gathering
- Design-requirements gathering
- Content/asset inventory
- User research/user-understanding efforts
- Notional success criteria definition

At this point, gathering the context for effective problem-solving requires elicitation from a wide variety of stakeholders, such as Product Owners and other business stakeholders. This is so the team understands the capabilities that a product should deliver. The team needs the involvement of technical stakeholders, such as a technical architect, to understand the solution constraints.

In Human-Centered Agile, the discovery activities also include elicitation from users, so that the team has a necessary understanding of user attitudes and behaviors, as well as the gathering of design constraints. This entire set of information forms the *problem definition* or the context for solution ideation. Without this information, teams may design infeasible or costly and ineffective solutions.

Finally, when considering the problem being solved, the team should consider how success will be defined and what the criteria for measuring success will be. At this early stage, teams should be thinking about what success looks like from the user and business standpoint so that as solutions are identified later, a measurement approach can be developed. One way to think about this is to use the definition of "outcomes" proposed by Jeff Gothelf and Josh Seiden:[1]

> An outcome is a change in human behavior that drives business results. Outcomes have nothing to do with making stuff—though they are sometimes created by making the right stuff. Instead, outcomes are the changes in customer, user, employee behavior that lead to good things for your company, your organization, or whomever is the focus of your work.

This definition is useful because it moves teams away from picking solutions and measuring success by measuring the amount of functionality built, replacing that with understanding how the products they build actually change someone's behavior.

The output of discovery is a well-articulated problem definition of the need that is being met through the following activities, with a defined **benefit hypothesis**, **value proposition**, and **success criteria**.

Ideation

Ideation and concept validation combine to ensure the right solution. In the Ideation step, teams explore and evaluate multiple solution concepts (often referred to as **lateral** or **divergent thinking**) and then select the solution path to be developed.

In software design, this may take place as a workshop or other collaborative exercise or as an asynchronous design activity where designs are reviewed by stakeholders. In this context, typical ideation deliverables include whiteboard diagrams or wireframes, user and screen flows, and so on. The team then evaluates these concepts for general feasibility and level

---

[1] Jeff Gothelf and Josh Seiden, 2019, *Outcomes Over Output*, Sense & Respond Press

of effort as part of deciding which solutions can move into the next step (concept validation).

Ideation can present a unique challenge for Designers on Agile teams as the design step often gets compressed into a single sprint, taking on the manner of "***satisficing***"—that is, the first solution that sounds good enough is the one that gets tried, with little time to explore alternatives. Often, work begins as a specific solution demanded from a Product Owner with no lateral thinking at all. In Human-Centered Agile, teams identify candidate solutions and apply user feedback as a factor toward selecting the best approach(es).

The output of ideation should be a small number of solution concepts, typically in an early ("low-fidelity") form. The team brings these concepts forward into concept validation to gain user feedback to determine which solution (if any) is successful and reflects the best approach for users.

NEW METHODS, FAMILIAR IDEAS

When discussing ideation, Human-Centered Agile values cooperation with business owners and key stakeholders (including users), bringing them into the collaboration space wherever possible. Recently, "design sprints" and "sprint zeros" have become popular methods for beginning collaborative ideation. This is meant to jump-start the creative process and ensure lateral thinking while also ensuring that business and technical constraints are considered.

It is important to recognize that, while the process has been updated, collaborative exploration, ideation, and prioritization sessions are far from new.

Prior to design sprints, joint application design (JAD), design charrettes, kaizen events, rapid application development (RAD), and many other specific methodologies were employed to encourage a team to collaboratively focus on specific problems with users. In point of fact, both HCD and Agile are heavily influenced by prior professional approaches.

Concept Validation

Concept validation ensures that users are included in the determination of whether a solution is worth delivering. Concept validation is perhaps the trickiest step to incorporate into Agile, where the "build it and see" philosophy demands a "Minimum Viable Product," or MVP. The usual practice is to assume that this means writing code. The philosophy of producing an MVP and seeking feedback from users is no different in Human-Centered Agile. However, in order to provide an MVP that is as lightweight as possible and still validates the team is building the right kind of solution, Human-Centered Agile recognizes that other kinds of prototypes and feedback gathering may work faster and cost less than code-based MVPs. For concept validation, even early **nonfunctional prototypes** (such as "click-through" static prototypes, wireframes, or even paper illustrations) are appropriate, as long as the user can clearly understand what they represent.

The output of concept validation is a decision to move forward with an intended solution; a specific "**pivot or persevere**" decision, using evidence, before investment becomes too great. In concert with a lateral thinking approach during ideation, this limits the risk of over-engineered solutions and of building expensive but unwanted "champion-driven" features.

The Delivery Cycle

The next three phases (refinement, development, and solution validation) are best understood as a cycle. In this cycle, **refinement** will be a familiar step for Agilists and includes story writing and estimation. Human-Centered Agile recommends that refinement includes a visual reference point (such as a wireframe or mockup) so that there is truly a shared understanding of what is being delivered. **Development**, as a phase, requires a slightly more expansive definition than is often recognized—building non-code prototypes that articulate interaction design and information architecture and that can be tested, falls into this category. **Solution validation** is the testing of a developed product (code or otherwise) with users.

The output of refinement is a set of actionable stories for developers or Designers to produce a testable product, which may be iterated upon further or released.

Refinement

Refinement ensures that the entire team has a shared understanding of what is going to be delivered. The refinement step begins when there is a clear enough agreed concept of what is to be developed that story writing can begin. Refinement, covering the time from story generation through story acceptance, is a familiar step for most Agilists already. In Human-Centered Agile, refinement typically includes a visual representation of the intended product. This ensures a shared understanding and provides the team with an opportunity to discuss assumptions and risks and uncover previously hidden considerations. Refinement also includes the identification of specific success measurements that can be used to evaluate how well a feature has solved the problem for users that was identified during discovery.

The output of refinement is a set of actionable stories for developers or Designers to produce a testable product, which may be iterated upon further or released.

Development

Development creates a product that can be tested or released. Development means any work to get to a testable product; in Human-Centered Agile, this may mean more refined designs, nonfunctional prototypes, and other models of the delivered product, with the purpose of learning in the fastest and least expensive way.

Even during code development, accepted stories and designs aren't always delivered exactly as intended. During development, technical assumptions get overturned, new exceptions are found, and teams learn that their acceptance criteria weren't perfect and may require a design update. Because this results in changes to what is delivered, it is crucial for Designers to remain available and engaged throughout delivery, so designs are updated while keeping the initial design goals and user outcomes in mind rather than focusing solely on technical expedience.

The output of development is a testable product.

Solution Validation

Solution validation is the work that a team does to make sure that the chosen solution is succeeding for users ("done right"). Solution validation can be done with code prior to release, or with prototypes that are at a high enough fidelity for usability testing. The team is gathering user feedback that is intended to highlight trouble spots and confusing experiences so that they can identify clear improvements to be made.

The output of solution validation is a set of bugs and improvements that are prioritized and, where necessary, addressed before product release.

Evaluation

Evaluation is the work that a team does to make sure that a released product is succeeding for users ("done right"). A common misconception about design thinking is that the process ends either at "deliver" or "test." The inference is that the design process is over when the thing is built and released. **Launch/release is not where the design process ends.**

No matter the rigor of testing and validation that has preceded a launch, there will be unpredicted outcomes. Users will have unexpected responses that create challenges. Some will be technical in nature, others will involve tool comprehension, feature findability/discoverability, or even just unanticipated responses to a product's aesthetic qualities. A product in the wild always performs differently than when it was validated in a controlled environment.

Actual users' post-release experiences determine the success or failure of the release. Understanding those experiences is critical to providing the insight needed to guide strategic investment in the product portfolio properly. Human-Centered Agile recognizes that getting this right requires understanding user attitudes and sentiment toward the team's products and their experience, not just measuring specific business-value metrics that often represent lagging indicators of value delivered.

The output of evaluation is an understanding of how your product is bringing value to users and, where it is lacking, to inform future product strategy.

HUMAN-CENTERED AGILE AND NEW PRODUCT DEVELOPMENT

At one point during the writing of this book, we showed our work to another author who asked us, "Is Human-Centered Agile used for new product development, or for established products that need iteration and maintenance support?"

The truth is that we hadn't anticipated this question, because we have used it for both. The easy response is that all the methods and practices in this book are suited to both. But in a sense, that answer is too glib, because while the methods are appropriate to both, the application is not *quite* the same. Specifically, the amount of work in each phase will differ based on what the team needs to learn in order to move forward confidently.

USING HUMAN-CENTERED AGILE
FOR IDEATING "BIG IDEAS"

In *Beyond the UX Tipping Point*,[2] Jared Spool talks about Disney's investment in the Magic Band, a concept that took a major investment from Disney to bring a concept (a single device that can make your visit seamless, and, yes, "magical") to life. The problem for Disney was well-understood. As Spool says in an article summarizing Disney's venture into UX:[3]

> Disney was struggling to provide great online experiences. In those days, guests trying to make reservations found the system confusing and difficult to use. It was common for someone trying to book a resort stay through the website to have to call the customer support center to complete the transaction.

Famously, Disney had to keep a bank of rooms free for customers that would book rooms at Disneyland but arrive at Disney *World*.

The part of the story that is interesting from a Human-Centered Agile lens is what they did next.

They started ideating on a big concept: The Magic Band. But they didn't do what a traditional Agile team might do—build a small piece of it, place it into use, and add to the experience from there (or, more to the point, to try to "iterate existing scattered pieces of the experience together"). In fact, that approach might not have worked to demonstrate and validate (and fund) a much more complex system of experiences. Instead, they modeled the experience—created fake bands, fake sensors, and experiential walkthroughs that made it clear what they were developing. The description of this process[4] does not leave one with the impression of a small, disposable model that could be learned from (e.g., to do concept validation). Compared to the final investment Disney would make in bringing the Magic Band to life, it was. They needed to be able to see that a big idea would actually make sense as a solution without building it first.

---

[2] www.youtube.com/watch?v=q374lg6RI-k
[3] https://articles.uie.com/beyond_ux_tipping_point/
[4] www.wired.com/2015/03/disney-magicband/

USING HUMAN-CENTERED AGILE

Carl Sagan opined that "[e]xtraordinary claims require extraordinary evidence."[5] The truth is that the more a team is planning to invest in something, the more that they will want to know that it is solving for an actual user need. Disney needed this. At different levels of maturity, products have differing needs for evidence and for the ideation process itself. Problems with complex solutions will require more work in discovery, ideation, and concept validation than frequent smaller iterations on well-understood products, whereby teams may devote more effort to the work of refinement and solution validation.

In the same article by Jen Cardello that suggests the "Right Problem, Right Solution, Done Right" framework, she classifies her team's work into five categories:

1. New product: Adding a new product to our portfolio to serve unmet needs of customers and prospects.
2. New capability: Adding a new workflow/feature/functionality into an existing product to meet the needs of customers.
3. UX debt: Redesigning an existing workflow/feature/functionality because it is not generating desired user behaviors, which is preventing us from meeting business objectives (i.e., acquisition, retention, operating costs).
4. Tech debt: Redesigning the UI because of underlying technology changes.
5. Optimization: Incrementally improving an experience to increase desired user behaviors and impact business outcomes.

Each of these different types of work is likely to require a different distribution of HCD efforts, because a team working on a new product will have different learning goals through their research and different creative opportunities than a team trying to improve an existing unsatisfactory experience. Human-Centered Agile accounts for this by planning and prioritizing research by aligning the size of research efforts to the learning goals of the team and the risk of moving forward *without* the research.

---

[5] *Cosmos*, 1980, BBC Television

Human-Centered vs. User-Centered . . . What's the Difference?

While some practitioners feel strongly about one term over the other, operationally there is no important distinction. During various phases of the process, teams interact with the people that use (or might use) their products to elicit their needs and desires and validate their solutions. "User experience" is a catchall term for all the parts of the design that impact how a user feels about it and that, when applied, may or may not incorporate user feedback at critical points.

Chapter 3

HCD Activities and Artifacts from Discovery through Concept Validation

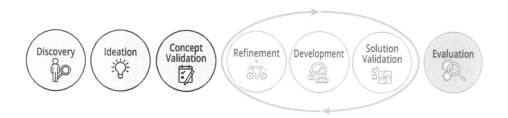

Each phase of Human-Centered Design (HCD) provides specific team-focused benefits (see Figure 3.1). It helps to understand the types of activities that occur in each phase and the specific purpose they serve so that practitioners can strategically integrate these activities into Agile delivery.

This chapter does not (and could not!) provide an exhaustive list of possible research techniques that can be employed in order to understand user attitudes and behaviors. These examples provide a starting point for understanding the activities that happen at each step, using some of the most common approaches.

The activities described here are geared toward the earliest phases of HCD, which are designed to make sure that teams are actually addressing user needs (right problem) in a useful way (right solution). These activities should lead teams to a pivot-or-persevere decision, paving the way to confidently move into delivery.

DOI: 10.4324/9781003188520-5

HCD Activities and Artifacts

DISCOVERY

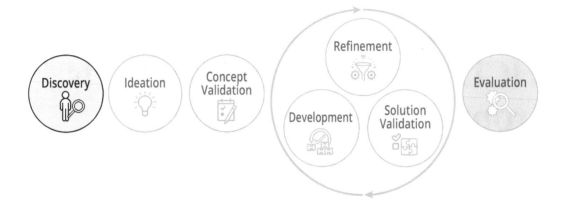

Example Activities

Research
Pluralistic walkthroughs/focus groups
Field observation/contextual inquiry
Individual sentiment gathering
   (e.g. interviews)
Indirect sentiment gathering
Digital ethnography

Design
Competitive/comparative review
Heuristic reviews
Gathering creative inputs
Creative workshops

Example Artifacts

Research
Personas
Empathy maps
Journeys maps
Service blueprints

Design
Heuristic score
Competitive/comparative analysis
Mood board and/or brand books
Creative brief
Style guides and pattern libraries
Problem definitions (as epics)

Purpose/ Activity

A clear problem definition
Problems have been validated by users
Team alignment on sprint and release goals
Product owner confidence

Figure 3.1 HCD activities and artifacts of discovery.

HCD and Discovery

During discovery, there are specific efforts that build an understanding of how the product is situated within the user's life and the context of usage, as well as what the user's attitude is toward the product and/or similar products. This research may be specific to an existing product already in use, allowing for observation of the behaviors around it, or it may be an understanding of the context and attitudes that inform how a user will react to a new product.

Either way, the goal is to understand whether people might value a specific product or feature and why, then learn how the team might increase that value. This is done before work is committed, because users can surprise even the most involved product teams.

From a team delivery standpoint, the discovery effort leads to a few key outcomes (see also Figure 3.1):

■ A clear problem definition
■ Problems have been validated by users
■ Team alignment on sprint and release goals
■ Product Owner confidence

A Clear Problem Definition

The team gains confidence in their ability to build a valuable solution through their discovery activities. Through these activities, they come to understand their users and develop ideas about what is wanted and needed and, specifically, how the team can provide a valuable solution. Without good problem definition, roadmaps tend to get set by whim, shiny objects, or hopeful guesses about what will make users find value. "If you build it, they will come" is a myth. Unlike the movie *Field of Dreams*, users rarely come just because products or features are built. A good problem definition also allows teams to develop outcome-based success criteria so that teams understand whether they have built a successful solution.

Problems Have Been Validated by Users

Once the team has an idea of what problems need to be solved for their users, they may take a step toward validating what they have learned. This validation builds confidence that their work will have value. This is typical when insights come indirectly, such as through some form of sentiment gathering or support ticket analytics.

Team Alignment on Sprint and Release Goals

It is hard to overstate how much value there is in clear, agreed-on overall goals and problem definitions. Being able to refer back to the core purpose of a release is valuable throughout refinement and delivery activities because, once the team is in the weeds of delivering specific functionality, it is easy to lose sight of the purpose.

Product Owner Confidence

Shifting from "hopeful guessing" to user-validated problems results in teams having increased confidence that their work will make a difference.

ACTIVITIES VS. ARTIFACTS

Often, when teams speak about the work of HCD, there is confusion between the activity being done and the artifact being generated. For example, interviewing users is an activity. These interviews may be codified into personas, which are artifacts.

Far too often, teams place an artifact on a roadmap without planning for the activities required to deliver it. This can be due to oversight but is more likely because those activities are not well understood by the team. For example, an artifact, such as persona or a journey map, will be placed on the roadmap, which will dutifully get assigned to an HCD practitioner without regard for its prerequisite activities (e.g., user interviews or workshops), assuming that the HCD practitioner can then work on their own to generate a quality deliverable. However, artifacts are research-driven. To make a good persona, journey map, or any other artifact that makes a statement about user attitudes, behaviors, or expectations, the HCD practitioner must actually engage with users at some point. Otherwise, they're merely presuming user attitudes and expectations, which does not add significant value.

When teams think about planning HCD activities, understanding the difference between activities and artifacts is key to understanding why they take a little longer to execute and need to be ahead of the rest of the roadmap. HCD activities include efforts such as recruiting users and then planning, conducting, and synthesizing research in time to bring that insight back into story refinement, which takes longer and requires additional organization and foresight than teams may be used to.

Additionally, the insights generated through HCD research are only valuable if teams have time to act on the findings. It doesn't matter if teams gather the most amazing insights in the world if the team doesn't have time to incorporate those insights into their decisions about the product.

Discovery Research Activities

The purpose of user research during discovery is to ensure that teams have an understanding of who their users are and what attitudes and expectations exist about the product and/or similar products—and gain a clear understanding of what Tony Ulwick and Clayton Christensen coined the "jobs to be done"[1,2] of whatever the team is building. This work goes a long way toward ensuring that teams are solving the right problem and provides the constraints, and sometimes suggestions, for the right solution.

The most common discovery research activities are:

- Field observation/contextual inquiry
- Pluralistic walkthroughs/focus groups
- Individual sentiment gathering
- Indirect sentiment gathering
- Digital ethnography

Field observation and contextual inquiry are merely different ways of saying that someone is observing users (or potential users) as they accomplish their tasks. It is ideal to do this in a setting as close to the user's natural context as possible although "direct observation" often occurs in labs or other controlled environments. Users are encouraged to "think aloud" or describe their attitudes and the reasons for their behaviors, and researchers record both the behaviors and the thoughts expressed by the user.

Pluralistic walkthroughs/focus groups are methods designed to collect feedback from more than one user at a single time. Pluralistic walkthroughs guide users through the experience, seeking feedback throughout the process. In this way, they are like a group version of contextual inquiry. Focus groups

---

[1] The History of Jobs-to-Be-Done and Outcome-Driven Innovation by Tony Ulwick, https://jobs-to-be-done.com/what-is-jobs-to-be-done-fea59c8e39eb
[2] Clayton M. Christensen and Michael E. Raynor, 2003, *The Innovator's Solution*, Harvard Business School Press

are more concentrated on attitudes than behaviors, since they take place after the fact and, in this way, are more like a collective version of a user interview.

Direct sentiment gathering is typified by one-on-one interviews and is a rich source of user attitudes. While these do not provide direct behavioral observation, the participant can report how they used the tool or whether they had specific problems. Interviews regarding direct experience with a tool are best conducted close to the user's intended experience so the participant's recollections are as fresh as possible, allowing the provision of direct examples based on experience.

USEFUL RESEARCH CONCEPTS

This book is mainly concerned with what types of research occur at which phases of the project lifecycle and how to integrate them into an Agile delivery process. It is not a primer on how to conduct research (or design, for that matter). However, there are some key concepts to understand when working with HCD practitioners that will improve discussions about what the team's research will look like:

■ Synchronous vs. Asynchronous and Moderated vs. Unmoderated
■ Remote vs. In Person and Field vs. Lab
■ Users vs. User Proxies

SYNCHRONOUS VS. ASYNCHRONOUS AND MODERATED VS. UNMODERATED

Synchronous vs. Asynchronous refers to whether someone will be watching and/or facilitating the research as the participant is going through it. Moderated vs. unmoderated differentiates whether someone is facilitating or guiding the experience. In practice, these two concepts usually go hand in hand. When moderating an experience, both the moderator and the participant need to be available at the same time. If unmoderated, an advantage is that it can be done asynchronously.

For example, say a team desires a usability test where a participant is asked to complete certain tasks while being observed and report their attitudes and reasons for their choices. This can be done in a moderated and synchronous way with an actual test administrator who might ask questions, help the user overcome specific blocks where necessary, and generally guide the process. However, these can also be done in an unmoderated, asynchronous way whereby tasks are set up to be done using online tools and users complete them without a facilitator. In these cases, behaviors are recorded for later analysis, and users may be prompted to answer planned questions.

REMOTE VS. IN PERSON AND FIELD VS. LAB

These days, it is quite common for moderated tests to be performed remotely since there are a number of tools available to support this. When tests are conducted in person, the researcher may travel to the subject in hopes of seeing them in their natural context or bring them into a more controlled environment, depending on the techniques called for.

When considering how valuable research will be, it's worth also correlating the fidelity of what is being observed to the actual experience that a user will have with the solution. As mentioned, the closer the research is to the user's reality, the better.

The researcher's quality of observation has a fidelity as well. In person, a researcher can gather high-quality feedback since they can see behaviors, body language, and facial expressions, or hear a tone of voice. This allows them to ask follow-up questions based on their observations. A researcher's fidelity is diminished when using remote participants, even more so when conducted asynchronously.

USERS VS. USER PROXIES

Fidelity is also applicable when considering the participants being tested. It is not always possible to have the actual users of a given solution contribute, so user proxies are used. Options for user proxies include:

■ Users with similar qualities
■ Support agents
■ Trainers
■ Other teams

Users with similar qualities can be used in certain situations. If user characteristics are known and current tool understanding is not a factor, proxies can be recruited outside of the user base. For example, if building a tool for tax preparers, tax preparation specialists that have relevant domain knowledge will suffice in the absence of the user base.

Support Agents are people that provide direct, daily support to users, such as a help desk or other tier 1 support providers. These people will have a good sense of what users do and do not like as well as where they struggle.

Trainers can also be good sources. If building solutions for a group of people that must take common training in the tools or adjacent areas, such as policies or professional support, trainers have a good sense of new users' perspectives.

Members of other teams can substitute these roles, if necessary, but this is often a last-ditch approach containing specific risks due to the likeliness of them being too familiar with the internal language and strategic goals. However, testing the solution with members from other teams is still valuable, if only to get "fresh eyes" and missing perspectives. This is an example of a very low-fidelity user proxy.

In all these cases, proxies are engaged in a way similar to the actual users. But remember that, while proxies are better than having no user representatives, they also introduce their own perspectives and may struggle to separate their user understanding from their own professional role. This is why they are thought of as low-fidelity user representatives.

The Product Owner is *not* a good user proxy. Rarely do Product Owners take it upon themselves to observe people using their product, and they are often invested in too many aspects of the solution to make a good proxy for what is being built. Even in those rare cases when they do, they are likely to have conflicting interests when it comes to representing what a user might want.

Discovery Research Artifacts

Research artifacts are the way that research is encoded and shared across teams, and insights are preserved for later use. They ensure that teams get the maximum benefit from the research activities conducted. During planning, it is important to remember that distilling the raw notes and records of activities into accurate and useful insights, a process called research synthesis, requires time. Imagine conducting 20 interviews—the research team doesn't hand off several dozens of pages of notes, nor do they just comment on their impressions during ideation and refinement. Instead, they aggregate the important findings into documents that express the insights that a team will need.

Personas and Empathy Maps

Personas are a description of common roles or types of users differentiated by factors that affect their attitudes or behaviors. They serve as information radiators about known user information, helping to focus conversations and product design decisions on developing new features with the understood user context in mind. Because of this, personas are most effective when they provide information that is likely to affect design decisions.

Some examples of information that impacts design are:

- How often do/might they use a product that accomplishes a specific purpose?
- Will they be everyday users that can be expected to learn and explore, or infrequent users that will need regular reorientation?
- What are their incentives for using the product?
- What is the context of their usage of the product? Where are they, what is competing for their attention, and so on?
- How well will this product fit within the habits and behaviors they already have?
- What are their likely alternatives or substitutes to the product?
- Which terms and language are they familiar with, and which will be new?

Empathy maps are related to personas and a visual representation of how a user feels when approaching or while engaging with the product or service being developed. Empathy maps tend to include less general contextual information, focusing more on the emotional state at the specific moment of engagement. While the potential for overlap between the information on a persona and an empathy map is great, they each still perform a useful communication function when getting a team aligned to figuring out the right solution.

A NOTE FROM THE DESIGNER ABOUT PERSONAS

"Mary is a 36-year-old Designer. She's also a mom on the go with little spare time."

At some point early in my career, personas had a moment. They became the artifact of choice, and customers started wanting them because they represented the fact that design was happening. However, the vast majority of the personas I saw created were basically little works of fiction—pictures and names of people that represented little more than a summary of the Product Owner's or product team's assumptions about a user.

As such, I became extremely skeptical of the value of personas. This was the beginning of my understanding that, in order to talk about design and what Designers do, we needed to separate activities from artifacts. I eventually learned to value personas specifically as the reason (some might even say the excuse) to do the interviews and other discovery activities that provide actionable insights.

Scenarios are key tasks users try to accomplish, complete with the context around the task, such as when or why a user is undertaking their action. There are often a few key scenarios that are particular to a user persona using a system, which are combined directly with personas, so that when teams are designing a solution, they have a picture of both who the user is as well as what they hope to accomplish.

Scenarios are distinguished from *use cases* mainly by the focus on user-specific emotions about getting a task done, expectations, and off-screen experiences. For example, a user may be asked, "What is likely to frustrate you as you try to accomplish task X?"

One classic design decision around scenarios is how likely the user is to actually *complete* an interaction in one sitting. Designing a data-entry form with users looks very different when it is a short form that has well-known information versus one that requires gathering information from multiple sources, which might take time.

Journey Maps and Service Blueprints

A journey map is an end-to-end breakdown of a process *as it appears to the user* even as other actors are involved and are enriched with attitudinal and behavioral observations. They note how many touchpoints the user encounters and what their expectations, frustrations, or delight points might be at each step. Journey maps are particularly useful for looking holistically at a process to identify areas for experience improvement, rather than simply looking at each encounter as a discreet experience. Service blueprints do much the same but expressly aim to fully identify "backstage" or "behind the curtain" parts of the holistic experience from the business's point of view.

Design Activities during Discovery

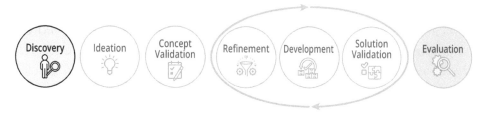

While the research activities of discovery are focused on understanding the user, there are a series of parallel design activities that should take place during discovery. Design activities are focused on understanding the design goals and constraints (for example, brand considerations) from the business's point of view as well as identifying opportunities for improvement based simply on best practices.

Heuristic Reviews

Heuristic reviews are expedient methods for problem-solving that use unconventional methods designed to arrive at a solution that is "close enough" given a very tight time constraint. A heuristic review is a professional review of an existing product or process that seeks to compare the process against general best practices, usually using a specific framework for what gets evaluated. Heuristic reviews use a common framework and are fundamentally subjective, so it is best to have more than one expert conduct the review and compare answers.

Competitive/Comparative Review

A **competitive** or **comparative** review is the evaluation of an existing or proposed product or process that seeks to compare it against similar processes using competitors as a key comparison point. The fundamental questions of a competitive/comparable review are along the lines of:

■ How are comparable organizations/products/processes addressing specific problems?
■ How do they present themselves?
■ What makes them successful and what challenges them?

Gathering Creative Inputs/Creative Workshops

Depending on the type of project and maturity of the solution, some discovery activity is likely to be focused on identifying brand-related goals of the product. Here, information is explored, such as whether incorporating existing design or identity materials (e.g., logo or other branding) is necessary if there is an existing brand book, or if it requires the use of approved colors, photographs, and the like. If these aspects of design are not already refined, they will also seek to learn the desired tone for the audience.

Because interactions with products are emotional as well as practical, if the product's identity is undefined, the team may wish to go through creative workshops or other exercises designed to elicit the design goals and values from an emotional or tonal perspective.

Design Artifacts during Discovery

For many of these activities, there is a one-to-one relationship between the activity and the artifact, which is why there is such frequent confusion between the two to begin with. These artifacts are still worth understanding as the deliverables of the activity itself. They include:

- Heuristic analysis/score
- Competitive analysis
- Mood board and/or brand book
- Creative brief
- Style guides and pattern libraries
- Early epic definition

Heuristic Score

The outcome of a heuristic review should be a document that scores the product against best practices, highlighting strengths and weaknesses. The scores should include analysis and suggestions for improvements that can often translate into the sort of quick wins that help a team's credibility.

Competitive/Comparative Analysis

The result of a competitive or comparative analysis is usually a breakdown of competitor products into strengths and weaknesses, which identifies conventions (i.e., patterns) in the ways that solutions are presented and delivered. This report is used to identify helpful conventions and opportunities for improvement, as well as gaps in what is being delivered, so that the team can find ways to deliver new value.

Mood Board and/or Brand Book

A mood board is a set of gathered materials (images, colors, other product examples) meant to serve as inspiration for the tone and style of the solution being developed. A brand book is a set of specific instructions about how a brand is represented throughout a product's marketing and development cycles. While they differ in how flexible they are (an inspiration board is a guide, a brand book is a set of visual constraints), their common purpose is to define the visual identity of a product.

Creative Brief

A creative brief is a document used to communicate the creative strategy of the product being built. It is a document containing details related to user understanding (i.e., who it is for, what the tone and style are, what the communications approach will be, what the key points of value differentiation are from a user perspective, etc.).

Style Guides and Pattern Libraries

A style guide is a product-specific set of established practices for delivery. For example, in software products, style guides define typography usage (typefaces, sizes, etc.), iconography usage, product colors (not just a palette of primary colors but a set of primary, secondary, and tertiary colors with specific instructions on where and how within the product those colors are used), button size, shape, and color, basic field appearance, commonly repeated values (such as dates), and perhaps specific interaction behaviors.

A pattern library is a collection of common styles used together. For example, a style guide may have specific definitions for how text fields are to be displayed, while a pattern library may define how address entries are handled (the order and labels of the fields, whether the zip code is five or nine digits, and even whether there is an address validation service). In practice, there is no perfect line between the two, but pattern libraries tend to be more robust. In either case, these are usually treated as living documents, and the team will have to make decisions about how to manage compliance with the guidance.

Problem Definitions (as Epics)

The purpose of discovery is to guide the generation of worthwhile problems to be solved for users. Once these problems are identified, they can be captured as epics, overarching units of work that are so large that they can take several months to deliver. They distill each of the specific problems to be solved into a single trackable place and describe this problem in terms of user value. This gives teams space to experiment with how to best solve the problem by building a small MVP to validate their concept and get early learning from users interacting with a real product in the field. This insight is key to helping teams pivot away from unsuccessful solutions early.

Epics break down into features that are medium-sized units of work that focus on delivering solutions to users. Features, in turn, break down into stories, which are much more granular than epics and are sized such that they can be completed in a single sprint (see Figure 3.2). During each sprint, teams focus on stories as the most granular unit of value delivery. User stories are small enough to complete in a single sprint but large enough to contain specific value to be delivered to the user through the story.

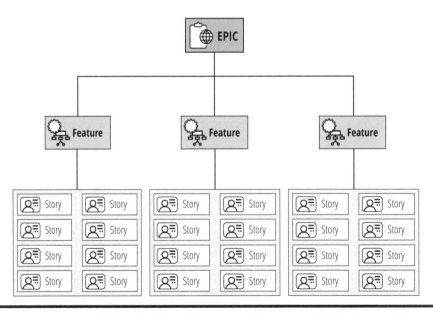

Figure 3.2 How an epic breaks down into many features, which, in turn, break down into multiple stories.

Epics also equip teams to answer the following questions:

1. "What is the problem that we are trying to solve for users, and what value do we expect them to receive?"
2. "Is this a problem that needs to be solved?"
3. "What are the "stakes?" (More on "stakes" in Chapter 6.)
4. "What is the benefit to the business of solving this problem?"
5. "What types of solutions are acceptable to users and feasible to deliver, at a level of effort appropriate to the problem?"
6. "How might the success of this solution be measured?"

HCD and Ideation

During ideation in Human-Centered Agile, the team generates competing solution concepts for further evaluation. This ensures that teams don't "over-engineer" solutions that are more complex or labor-intensive than the value the solution returns. When possible, ideation is done collaboratively with users so that the team is directed toward creating experiences that are more likely to be successful.

The goal of ideation is to ensure that the team uses a good understanding of the problem to be solved to identify solutions that will be effective for users and successful for the business.

From a team delivery standpoint, collaboration and lateral thinking during ideation leads to a few key outcomes (see also Figure 3.3):

■ Consideration of multiple ***solution candidates*** up front
■ Shared understanding of the solution candidate selection criteria
■ Shared understanding of experience goals, risks, and trade-offs of solution candidates
■ Product Owner confidence and team buy-in

Multiple Solution Candidates

Too often, teams receive direction in the form of a specific requested solution, possibly from leadership or other stakeholders. Without a step that determines whether this request fits a validated problem (right problem) or whether this solution is a good fit in terms of user expectations or level of effort and considers alternative solution candidates, the team is at much greater risk of producing unwanted or over-engineered solutions.

HCD Activities and Artifacts

IDEATION

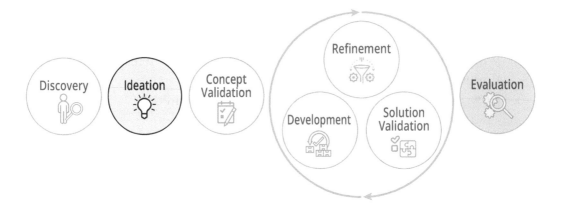

	Research	Design
Example Activities	Informal knowledge transfer Insight share-outs Direct workshop participation	Collaborative design workshops Experience risk evaluation Independent design
Example Artifacts	*None*	Storyboard Screen/user flows Wireframes

Purpose/Activity
Multiple solution candidates
Solution candidate selection criteria
Experience goals, risks, and trade-offs

Figure 3.3 HCD activities and artifacts in ideation.

Solution Candidate Selection Criteria

A team that knows why they are building a solution is going to have a clearer sense of purpose and understanding about delivering that solution. Collaborative ideation allows team members to know which competing solution candidates were considered and why they were ruled out. Teams that have had a chance to explore the *what* and the *why* get derailed less easily by lingering doubt over the solution path that has been selected.

Experience Goals, Risks, and Trade-Offs

Because solution selection is a collaborative process, solutions are considered with multiple criteria in mind. Having the right contributors means that risks can be identified and addressed early and that solutions that are high risk can be ruled out as appropriate. This also means that when teams move into development, future decisions can be made with reference to known risks so that they are addressed along the way.

Product Owner Confidence

Each of the phases from discovery through concept validation is intended to give the product team, and the Product Owner, confidence that they are solving the right problem and that they are getting to the right solution. Collaborative ideation means that Product Owners have more confidence that a range of solutions has been considered and that there is not a better solution that never got considered.

Research Activities during Ideation

Ideation consumes research information that was generated during discovery. Ideation doesn't produce new research insights; however, it is crucial to ensure that insights generated by the researchers are available and *actually get used* by the team. How this happens depends on the size of the team and the size of the effort.

During this phase, the research team is likely to participate in one of two ways:

- **Informal knowledge transfer**—On smaller teams, and especially when the researcher and the Designer are the same practitioner, knowledge transfer is often informal, largely happening during story refinement and other communication points with the Product Owner and/or other team members. While there may not be a specific activity devoted to sharing the insights gained with the rest of the team, it is still a good practice to think about how to codify and share research insights to be as effective as possible. This ensures that they remain valuable as teams grow, team membership changes, or simply as time goes by.

- **Insight share-outs**—For larger teams, or where research is separated from design, it can be necessary to plan specific meetings to explain and answer questions about insights generated and how they might impact the product being built. Along with the delivered research artifacts, this keeps user knowledge at the forefront of the decision-making process about what to build.
- **Direct workshop participation**—When ideation is done through collaborative workshops, members of the research team should be full participants. Through their participation, they act as an advocate for users, informed with research insights.

Design Activities during Ideation

Ideation is the phase during which teams generate multiple *high-level* solution concepts. These concepts need to be robust enough for the team to do a rough evaluation of the effort and risk of each solution candidate and to decide which solution candidates to validate with users. This is so the team can make informed decisions about which solution is the best fit for the problem being solved. At this point, the big picture of the solution is clear, but the details may not be.

There are fundamentally two paths that teams choose when trying to get to agreement on the basic design of a product—collaborative design workshops and conceptual designs.

Collaborative Design Workshops

In this scenario, the Designer works with other stakeholders (sometimes including users themselves) to collectively brainstorm solution possibilities. Workshops can vary a great deal in structure and duration, but the goal is to give teams and stakeholders a shared understanding of the purpose of the solution and problems to be solved and then to set them loose creatively (within whatever constraints apply) in solving those problems.

Independent Design

In this scenario, the Designer works independently using discovery artifacts to create design approaches that are presented to the Product Owner and team for feedback. At this design stage, major/key steps are considered and limited to so-called happy path activities (without exploring edge cases or error handling). The solution concepts are clear enough to initiate discussions and begin receiving feedback about the level of effort required for delivery and overall user value.

Experience Risk Evaluation

One of the advantages of collaborative ideation, which includes multiple stakeholders, is that experience risks emerge early. Human-Centered Agile practitioners are focused on risks regarding whether a team is building unwanted or unsatisfying solutions, but collaborative ideation also promotes early awareness of other risks (technical risks, policy risks, etc.) that can surface and be captured and addressed.

PRO TIP FROM THE DESIGNER: KNOW YOUR DESIGN SOCIALIZATION PATH

As obvious as this sounds, each stakeholder reacts differently to designs, coming to design reviews with varying, fundamental interests and abilities to "see" what is meant when being presented with a design that is less than fully mature.

DIFFERENT LEVELS OF ABSTRACTION

Some stakeholders are uncomfortable evaluating a design before knowing everything about it. For example, the stakeholder may need to see a high-fidelity mock-up (or even a prototype) to understand how the specific interactions will work before being comfortable agreeing to specific design decisions. Other stakeholders can look at a whiteboard drawing and internalize the direction and likely complications of a design at nearly a glance—enough to have a shared understanding with the team of what the delivered design will be.

Who designs are shown to—which stakeholders, at what specific fidelity and maturity, and in what order—is an under-recognized aspect of getting the design process right. The goal is to prevent too much work being spent on a design that any particular stakeholder can veto after it is in a mature state. Some stakeholders feel left out of the process if they see a mature design they did not have a say in, while others do not want to weigh in until something is mature enough to feel close to a decision to approve or disapprove. (The risk in doing a great deal of work just to get to the point where an Executive feels comfortable saying "no" is so common that it has a name: "executive swoop and poop.") What's more, the type of stakeholder (e.g., leadership, technical architect, Product Owner) doesn't always indicate who is going to want to see designs during their ideation and validation.

Teams often think there is an objectively correct order to designs—for example, sketching before doing the wireframes that precede mock-ups. In practice, it is crucial for stakeholders to see the design ideas *at the time* and *in the manner* where they can best provide meaningful feedback. Otherwise, the risk of doing too much work ahead of getting critical buy-in, only to have it discarded by a stakeholder can increase.

Here is an example of a common socialization path.

1. Collaboratively create a notional design with business/requirements analysts—a low-fidelity sketch of screens and screen flow.
2. Show developers to open the discussion about key technical risks or constraints.
3. Show the Product Owner to open the discussion about suitability to goals.
4. Refine the design through the story iteration process, involving all stakeholders.

There can also be paths that involve working collaboratively with the Product Owner right from the start, which means showing the Product Owner before developers. In many ways, who a design is shown to first rests largely on which stakeholders have the greater tolerance for the uncertainty that comes from the upstream portion of the creative process.

Design Artifacts of Ideation

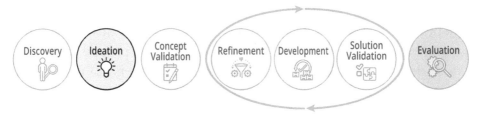

A **storyboard** (and its cousin, the comic) is a narrative description of the solution to be developed, supported by sample or low-maturity visuals that represent how a user is moving through the process. The value of the storyboard is that it is easy to understand and share as a solution concept and explicitly includes the user and their thinking as part of the description of the solution. As a side benefit, narrative explanation can spark further imagination and exploration work.

Screen/user flows are similar to storyboards but are presented from a product perspective rather than in a narrative format. Screen flows (or user flows) are a step-by-step sequence of screens or other interaction touchpoints that will take the user from intended action(s) to completed action(s). The value of a screen flow is that teams can dive slightly deeper into how the solution works, using the platform it is being created on (e.g., mobile devices, computer screens, point-of-sale interfaces, etc.).

Wireframes are a low-fidelity version of the screen. At this stage, these can range from whiteboard or pen-and-paper drawings to higher-fidelity renderings but are still low in design maturity.

MATURITY, FIDELITY, AND PROXIMITY

Maturity, fidelity, and proximity are three key concepts used by Designers when presenting their work to help orient stakeholders to what discussions are worth having when reviewing an in-progress design effort.

Maturity is a description of the amount of work and thought that has been put into a given design. In Agile, a team member might define maturity by considering how well-refined a story is and determining if it is "ready" to be worked on.

During ideation, teams should ask questions such as:

▪ What problem(s) is this design solving?
▪ What alternatives have we considered?
▪ What is the overall complexity, and what are the greatest design risks in this solution? (For example, does the design have technical risks that have not been addressed? Are there experiential concerns that require validation?)
▪ What will testing this look like?

In the early stages, these conversations drive decisions about the stakes of the design, and how much research is still required to make a good decision to move forward.

By contrast, during refinement, teams should ask questions such as:

- Does the design fit into any required standards and use expected design patterns?
- Has the design considered the full set of interactions necessary and/ or available to the user?
- Has the Designer considered how well the design will handle exceptions?
- Has the design been discussed with technologists to account for constraints?
- Have different states of the design been considered, including feedback to user actions (which includes not just user or system errors but also success indicators, warnings, and informational prompts)?
- Will the design scale if the amount of content it supports changes, and so on?

If these questions haven't been sufficiently answered, the design is not ready for development and needs further refinement to address them.

Fidelity refers to how close, visually, the design is to the final product intended for release. Fidelity ranges from very low (napkin drawings, whiteboard sketches) to wireframes and mock-ups. This is particularly important to describe when teams are using well-established style guides and visuals as part of their initial designs. Refined visuals can make it seem as though the ideas represented are more mature than they are; polished visuals easily get confused for polished ideas.

Proximity describes how quickly the design is expected to be picked up for implementation and delivered. The shorter the time frame, the narrower the scope of changes that can be made to the design gets.

These concepts are important, because design critique answers different questions during different phases of Human-Centered Agile. Early ideation is about creating and evaluating solution concepts—the designs tend to be both low maturity and ***low fidelity***, which is appropriate for getting to agreement on what is worth making. With delivery in the distance, teams can consider the general value of ideas.

Refinement and solution validation require more mature and higher-fidelity designs, so that teams can determine whether the details of execution are correct and generate a shared understanding of what is actually going to be delivered. When moving from refinement to development, the "correct" fidelity is a negotiated relationship between the Designer and the Agile team. Some features/stories need low fidelity; others need high fidelity. When fidelity is too low, teams end up fixing work that wasn't as a key stakeholder (usually, a Product Owner) had in mind. When it is too high, the amount of time in refinement is higher than it should be for the actual work being produced.

HCD and Concept Validation

During concept validation, the team reviews conceptual designs with users, to ensure that solutions are addressing user needs in a useful way. If multiple solution candidates are under consideration, gathering user attitudes toward each also allows for a better decision on which solution will provide the best experience. These efforts ensure that teams spend time working on products that users want and understand.

Concept validation is a research step—neither an HCD practitioner nor an Agile team can validate that their intended solution is successful without engaging their users. Deciding which research to undertake is also a "stakes-based" process; the amount of effort put into solution validation should align with the investment a team will make in delivering that solution and the risk of delivering something unwanted or ineffective.

From a team standpoint, concept validation leads to two key outcomes, including (see also Figure 3.4):

- A "pivot or persevere" decision based on evidence
- An early signal of experience risks or challenges

A Pivot or Persevere Decision

Just as ideation ensures the team considers multiple solutions to any problem they are trying to solve, concept validation provides a natural step for a pivot-or-persevere. During ideation, teams compared the business value and technological level of effort of different solutions; here, they get enough user input to make a good decision about whether they are creating good experiences that support their goals.

HCD Activities and Artifacts
CONCEPT VALIDATION

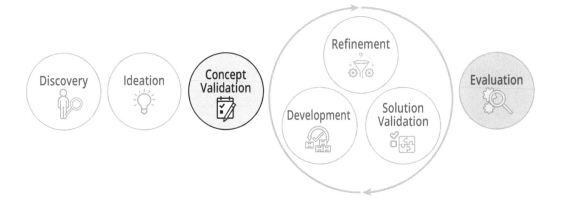

Example Activities	**Research**
	Identify learning goals
	Prepare research efforts
	Recruit participants
	Conduct research

Example Activities

Research
Identify learning goals
Prepare research efforts
Recruit participants
Conduct research
   Impression tests
   Paraphrase tests
   Card sorting
   Task completion tests
   Feature ranking

Design
Design refinement
Prototype construction

Example Artifacts

Research
Test plans
Test script
Test data
Summary of findings

Design
Paper mock-ups
Low-fidelity prototypes
Updated insight repository

Purpose/ Activity
A pivot or persevere decision
Identified experience risks or challenges

Figure 3.4   HCD activities and artifacts in concept validation.

An Early Signal of Experience Risks or Challenges

Even in cases where teams get a clear signal that it is worth moving forward, the team may uncover risks that need to be addressed further along in the refinement stage. Are there specific concepts, labels, or interactions that are unclear? Does it take more work than expected to explain what the intended value of a solution is? What types and levels of risk can the team accept and still be confident they have identified the right solution?

"PIVOT OR PERSEVERE"

In his book *The Lean Startup*, author Eric Reis coined the term "pivot or persevere" for the decisions teams and organizations frequently make in the build–measure–learn cycle of new product development. Teams often ask questions, such as:

- "Should we keep going down this path, or give up and try a new one?"
- "Did that Minimum Viable Product (MVP) prove our hypothesis?"
- "Is there an alternative method for getting us where we need to go"
- "Are we getting the benefits we had hoped to achieve from this work?"

Teams constantly ask themselves these questions as they progress through the cone of uncertainty toward an optimal solution. The idea, of course, is to pivot away from what is not working toward an alternate solution when necessary.

The whole point is to give teams the ability to pivot away from a suboptimal solution toward a solution or approach that works better before too much time and money has been spent. In the case of a "failed" solution, the result is not "thrown away" but rather used as a learning experience for one suboptimal approach. Even successful solutions are evaluated for possible areas of improvement as teams continuously measure, learn, and improve in the Lean Start-Up Cycle.

IGNORE SUNK COSTS

In economics, a sunk cost is an expense that has already been incurred and cannot be changed. Product Owners and Product Managers are strongly encouraged to ignore sunk costs when making budgetary decisions. Often, managers will reason that they've spent too much time or money already and cannot change the plan, despite evidence and results suggesting otherwise.

Be vigilant about the sunk-cost fallacy as teams proceed in their work. The project that has incurred $1,000 (or even $1,000,000) in costs is not a reason to "expect a win" or to justify its continuation in the face of data that dictates otherwise.

Research Activities of Concept Validation

In concept validation, the team uses early-stage designs (sometimes in the form of paper prototypes or other low-fidelity versions) with potential users for direct feedback. The amount of work it can take to do this varies greatly, depending on how much existing research operations support there is, and how extensive the research itself is. When coordinating both concept validation and solution validation research, teams will want to use a Research Roadmap (see Chapter 7) to ensure that there is enough time and alignment between research and development work.

Identify Learning Goals

The first task of any research effort is to identify specific learning goals. It is not usually enough to merely show something and "get feedback"—it is important that the team consider what it is actually hoping to learn. At the concept validation stage, these will be big-picture questions that take the form of questions such as:

- Do users understand what we are making and how it will help them?
- What is their attitude toward the type of solution we are considering?
- What are the risks or challenges that they might experience when faced with this solution?

Prepare a Research Effort

Once a learning goal is established, the team will prepare for the research effort. This means picking the methodology that works best. In addition to selecting a method best suited to answer the learning goals, additional factors may include what type of tools teams have access to and whether they can devote time and have access to direct interaction with users via moderated tests (whether in person or remote).

There are a wide number of testing methodologies aimed at understanding different aspects of how the user will interact with the solution. Each method tests for a specific kind of insight, and methods are not universal in the type of prototype or model required to conduct the test. The following list is not an exhaustive list of research methodologies. For an approachable and useful rundown of research methodologies, read Erika Hall's *Just Enough Research*.[3] A few examples follow:

---

[3] Erika Hall, 2013, *Just Enough Research*, A Book Apart

- **Impression Tests:** A user is shown representations of key interaction points (such as a home page) and asked what they understand to be the purpose and behaviors of what they see. This helps teams understand whether the arrival experience is clear for users and whether users have a clear idea of next steps and anticipated value. The latter is used to gather attitudinal feedback on the expected value that a team is delivering.
- **Paraphrase Tests:** A user is asked to restate their understanding of what the experience is offering. This test is specific to the language used, whether as labels for content or navigation or for an explanation and description that the user needs to understand.
- **Card Sorting:** A user is asked to organize information in ways that are relevant to them. Depending on the specific methodology, this may also include adding their own expected content types and titling content groups. This method is particularly useful for understanding user mental models of complex content structures or interaction sets.
- **Task Completion Tests:** The user is shown an end-to-end representation of a solution and asked to accomplish something very specific. This method is useful to see how easily they go from start to finish. During concept validation, this method is seeking to understand whether there is a good fit between the intended experience and the outcome the user needs.
- **Feature Ranking:** A user is asked to rank multiple potential solutions to be delivered by a product. This method is good for understanding and validating user interest in specific features, particularly for prioritization purposes. This method can also reveal red flags in proposed features.

Preparing for any of these efforts will include identifying the tools being used for the test, generating a test script, and planning a reporting methodology that is suited to the audience of the results.

Recruit Research Participants

Recruitment is not to be underestimated as one of the heaviest lifts in any research effort. The team needs to identify the appropriate participant characteristics (e.g., teams creating something geared toward first-time users won't want to test with experienced users).

For moderated tests, those candidates need to be contacted, scheduled, and granted access to whatever testing platforms are being used all need to

be accounted for. Some organizations will have a separate research operations team to handle this work; for those that do not, this step should not be
taken for granted. Finally, anyone scheduling sessions needs to remember
that facilitators and note-takers need time to prepare ahead of a session and
time to consolidate notes after a session.

Conduct Research Efforts

Conducting the research effort might mean setting up an asynchronous test,
in which case this step requires little work; monitoring participation; and
supporting participants if they have questions or issues. If the research effort
includes any moderated or in-person time with users, it will take more time.
It is also beneficial to include not just HCD practitioners in this step—when
other team members act as notetakers and observers, their participation also
reinforces the idea that creating good outcomes is a team responsibility, and
the insights resonate across the entire team.

Synthesize Research Findings

Finally, collecting and analyzing results is an effort that takes time; raw
results may be interesting but are not useful for most stakeholders without
analysis. The HCD practitioners doing this will need to know what deliverable is expected, who the audience is, and what decisions are being supported. With this information, the team can effectively report their insights.

Research Artifacts of Concept Validation

Test Plan: This is the document that describes the purpose and methodology of the test itself and should be in place by the time any research is
kicked off. The test plan captures the learning goals and the methodology used. It can also include logistics, such as the recruitment strategy and
scheduling information.

   Test Script: For moderated research, having a script orients participants
to the research session, giving them an understanding of what they are
about to do and why. It also ensures that the team is gathering data properly
across all their participants—for example, that the same questions are being
asked in the same way. This makes the data more consistent and useful during synthesis.

Test Data: Whatever is method used, there is a set of raw data that is captured from the research. This set might be interview notes, participant results from a card sort, or raw survey numbers.

Insights: The synthesis process produces insights—the individual, actionable observations that get used to make product design decisions.

Summary of Findings: In addition to specific insights, almost every research effort produces summarizing documentation—a narrative explanation of what was learned, including supporting evidence. There can be multiple summaries from a single effort (e.g., an executive summary *and* a detailed report, depending on the audience addressed and their needs).

Design Activities and Artifacts during Concept Validation

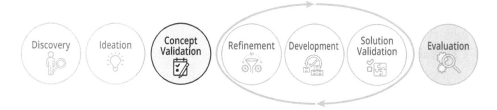

Because concept validation is primarily a research activity, design activity is limited to any design refinement that is required for the prototypes being tested. Designers need to make sure that any designs have enough information for test participants to understand and provide meaningful feedback.

Design Refinement

The designs for solution candidates that came out of ideation should have created a shared understanding within the team. This does not necessarily mean they will be understandable for users or ready for research. There can still be design work required to create a product suitable for users that can be used for testing and organizing the designs as needed by the test methodology. For example, these changes might include changing the fidelity of the design so that the users have enough context, the language and content being shown to better match user vocabulary or creating a series of specific screens to represent a specific interaction to validate that users understand how the solution is intended to work.

WHAT COUNTS AS A PROTOTYPE?

"Prototype" is one of those words that gets used a lot in a variety of contexts. Any early model of a product could be considered a prototype, but, in product development, the term usually refers to something that a stakeholder can interact with in a way that represents the intended experience. For simplicity, it is useful to think of prototypes falling into two categories: design prototypes and developed prototypes.

DESIGN PROTOTYPES

Design prototypes don't require coding, new hardware features, and the like. For example:

- **Paper prototypes**—As the name suggests, these are constructed and interacted with physically (usually with paper, but transparencies or blocks may also be used).
- **Clickable wireframes or mock-ups**—There is now a wide array of tools that let users navigate to a website or set of local files and click-through-linked (but otherwise static) screens in a way that resembles expected use cases.
- **Walkthrough experiences**—These are live simulations of the way that a user might move through an experience to understand their attitudes and behaviors.

DEVELOPED PROTOTYPES

Developed prototypes are code-based models of the intended product. These don't need to be nearly completed ("beta") products, but they are typically more full-featured and present more realistic product behaviors than design prototypes. For example, the user should be able to click and interact with a wider array of functionality and do things, like direct data entry, rather than taking steps that mimic data entry.

WHAT MAKES A GOOD PROTOTYPE?

Any prototype can make a useful testing experience. Design prototypes allow a team to test whether the product is easily understood, whereas developed prototypes allow testing to be conducted on a wider range of aspects. Teams can then reorganize information and present it to users in a way that makes sense to them by improving features, like navigation, labeling, and information display. Teams can also ensure participants have accurate expectations of how the product will behave and test basic design interaction. All these tests help to validate the "right solution."

Some examples of common, testable questions at this point include:

- Is the page organization easily understood?
- Are labels and instructions clear and comprehensive?
- Are the calls to action (e.g., buttons) clear and findable?
- What does the participant expect will happen when they take specific actions, such as clicking a link or pressing a button?
- Does the overall screen flow and organization make sense?

From a developed prototype, test "done right" questions, like:

- Are the interactions, transitions, and feedback clear enough during user activity?
- Is the user actually going where and doing what was expected?
- Are there gaps in what users are trying to do and what the system allows?
- Do users take longer than expected to complete the task? Do they get frustrated?

Obviously, the more mature and higher fidelity the prototype, the more robust the insights will be. The trade-off here is that lower-fidelity prototypes are cheaper, faster, and easier to make. A shared goal of Agile and HCD is learning what will be successful in the earliest and cheapest possible ways—early tests of conceptual designs can prevent expensive or unnecessary tests (or prototypes or releases).

Chapter 4

HCD Activities and Artifacts from Refinement through Evaluation

This chapter describes the team-focused benefits provided by Human-Centered Design (HCD) once the team has chosen solutions to deliver. It helps to understand the types of activities that occur throughout the overall delivery process, which includes refinement and solution validation, and the specific purpose these activities serve.

The activities are designed to make sure that teams are delivering their solution in a clear and usable way (done right). These activities should help teams find gaps and issues that users encounter, allowing them to lower the risk of costly issues at release, and inform their improvement and maintenance as they look forward.

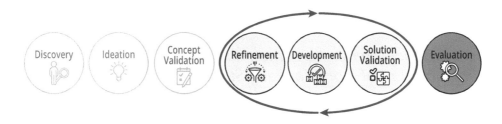

DOI: 10.4324/9781003188520-6

HCD and Refinement

During refinement, the team comes to a clear, shared understanding of what exactly is going to be delivered to users. For teams working in Agile, refinement is already a familiar activity, in the form of story writing and refinement.

From an HCD perspective, refinement focuses on identifying and making any remaining design decisions that will get picked up by the team for implementation and providing any visual references needed to support story understanding and agreement. Additionally, during refinement teams identify the specific ways in which their solutions will be measured for success during evaluation.

Previously generated research artifacts are consumed by the team during refinement so that decisions get made with users in mind. Otherwise, research activity is limited to any participation researchers take in story writing and refinement as part of the team.

From a team standpoint, refinement using visual reference documentation leads to some key outcomes beyond typical refinement (see also Figure 4.1):

■ Teams are more likely to identify gaps before starting.
■ Stronger Product Owner agreement and a clearer definition of done for each story.
■ Teams have a clearly defined outcome-based success measurement approach.

Teams Are More Likely to Identify Gaps before Starting

One of the benefits of teams visually representing the work that is going to happen is that teams are more likely to find gaps in the interaction design of a solution. Teams identify additional features that users will need, and consider less obvious cases, once a realistic representation of the solution is in front of them.

Stronger Product Owner Agreement and a Clearer Definition of Done for Each Story

The other benefit of visual representation is that the Product Owner has a clear sense of what will be delivered, which minimizes the number of times a team hears, "That's not what I meant." There is less time spent in refinement getting to agreement than if the team builds a product only to have to iterate to achieve the Product Owner's intended outcome.

HCD Activities and Artifacts

REFINEMENT

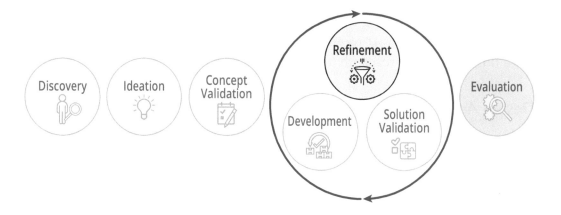

	Research	Design
Example Activities	*Participation in agile events*	Design refinement Content generation/revision Design standards review and updates
Example Artifacts	**Research** *None*	**Design** Content Wireframes Mockups Acceptance criteria Style guide and pattern library updates

....

Purpose/ Activity Teams are more likely to identify gaps before starting
Stronger product owner agreement and a clearer definition of done
    for each feature
Teams have a clearly defined outcome-based success measurement approach

Figure 4.1   HCD activities and artifacts in refinement.

Teams Have a Clearly Defined Outcome-Based Success Measurement Approach

The team determines what kinds of metrics and signals are appropriate to learn whether the solution has had the intended impact on users. They then create stories for gathering those metrics during evaluation. This work is a team activity, so it doesn't require specific design or research activities at this stage but will impact research activities downstream.

Design Activities of Refinement

Design refinement takes many forms, but the goal is essentially the same—to give the team a shared understanding of what is to be delivered by articulating all design details. This includes its visual elements, the expected behaviors (including specific interaction behavior), feedback messaging, and any other aspect of the solution a user will experience while engaged. It is highly recommended that for all but the smallest of stories, visual references are provided for the work being delivered.

Content generation/revision is crucial to success. Any content required by the solution needs to be created or reviewed during the refinement process. This includes any copy that is part of the experience and pieces of content related to interaction (field labels, hint text, etc.) and feedback during interactions.

Design standards review and updates are part of the collaborative process. Even within a single team, it is often necessary to maintain a style guide and pattern library to ensure product consistency, which is especially true for products with a long life cycle and frequent updates. Designs for upcoming stories should be reviewed against existing standards, and new styles/patterns should be incorporated when they are required.

Design Artifacts of Refinement

Content

It is important that content be considered a product worthy of review and refinement in equal standing to code, interaction design, and visual design. Every aspect of usability relies, to some degree (and often to its largest degree), on how well the content works: wayfinding, orientation, and decision support all depend on good labels, clear descriptions, meaningful feedback, and so on. Teams should be looking to ensure that content is concise and written in language that is familiar to the user, in addition to matching the intended tone.

It is possible to test for content usability just as any other sort of usability, and content testing should lead to refinement as all usability testing does.

Furthermore, any copy seen by a product's user needs to be documented in such a way that the team can deliver it accurately. This seems like a simple point, but it is worth pointing out that teams sometimes struggle to ensure that content is referenced properly by the delivery team.

Wireframes, Mock-Ups . . . and Acceptance Criteria

There is not one specific, right deliverable to generate shared expectations of what the design will deliver. Shared understanding can be accomplished through wireframes, mock-ups, screenshots that are annotated, or even just well-written stories. Visual references give teams an advantage because they decrease miscommunication when there might be multiple interpretations of written criteria. The important outcome is that the team's output matches a set of shared expectations, and the team avoids having "that's not what I meant" conversations with the Product Owner or other stakeholders.

The difference in wireframes, or any other visuals, in this phase compared to those mentioned earlier in the process is their maturity. When stories are refined, wireframes may need to be updated to demonstrate specific, additional interactions not initially considered to account for technical constraints that emerge. Mock-ups are not always needed in the refinement stage. They are generated to finalize the visual designs for new products and features or incorporate new visual design elements into the product. Put another way, a story changing from radio buttons to a drop-down menu doesn't need a mockup, but a story adding a new "wizard" for collecting information usually does.

Style Guide and Pattern Library Updates

Any new styles required or design patterns identified should be updated in the style guide, pattern library, or any other governing documentation as soon as they are agreed on for implementation.

EVALUATING DESIGNS

When engaging in design, it's important to exclude emotions. "I like/don't like it" isn't a useful framework for figuring out whether the design is any good. The goal is to decide whether the *user* will like it.

"WHAT PROBLEM ARE WE TRYING TO SOLVE?"

At the beginning of Chapter 2, design was described as the intentional creation of a specific experience or outcome.

Another way to think about design in the context of solution delivery is to ask what problem the Designer is trying to solve. Without a problem statement or description of the intended outcome, it is virtually impossible to evaluate how successful a design is. A Designer should be able to articulate the purpose of their design by describing:

- How the audience is supposed to feel
- What the audience is supposed to learn
- What is assumed to be understood already
- What primary action someone is expected to take and if there are secondary actions
- What specific attitudes or behaviors the design is trying to encourage and how

When evaluating a design, there are a few questions that may help focus discussion away from a "like it/don't like it" conversation. Here are two examples.

"WHAT TRADE-OFFS ARE BEING MADE IN THIS DESIGN?"

When reviewing a design, teams may find it beneficial to discuss the specific trade-offs being made. A "clean" design, with lots of white space and fewer visual elements, does a great job of focusing attention on specific content or calls to action but may hide high-value features that don't adhere to the design. By contrast, a design that includes too many elements or possible user actions may impose a high cognitive burden on a user, making it difficult to know what is important or the general purpose of the solution. Likewise, raising the profile of an element within the visual hierarchy means drawing attention away from every other element of the page.

"WHAT ARE THE RISKIEST PARTS OF THIS DESIGN?"

The goal of this question is to identify the parts of the design connected to its goal that the team is least comfortable with. That is to say, if a design is trying to accomplish a specific outcome, what parts of the design are most likely to get in the way of that? Examples can be unclear guidance, ill-suited tone, or even elements that are hard to find. The less mature the design, the more valuable this question is.

HCD and Development

During development, the team ensures that the solution being built matches the stories that have been written. From a design and research perspective, the specific activity is focused on review and, when needed, any in-flight adjustments that are required. This is primarily a design step, although it is possible for the team making an in-flight design update to seek relevant existing research insights.

From a team standpoint, development support leads to two key outcomes (see also Figure 4.2):

- Releasable products, produced as expected
- In-flight decisions/adjustments that reflect design intent

Releasable Products, Produced as Expected

Along with creating a visual reference (such as a mock-up or wireframe), having the Designer review stories for completion assures that they are completed as agreed and expected. This includes making sure that everything looks and feels as described in the story or acceptance criteria and that delivered products match established style guides and design patterns.

In-Flight Decisions/Adjustments That Reflect Design Intent

It is common for developers to run into unexpected issues during development, such as unexpected technical constraints or new exceptions that weren't documented. Adjustments to design are best handled by collaboration between the Designer and developers so that the best possible alternative can be found that incorporates the user's needs and matches the design intent.

Design Activities of Development

In-flight design support is any work the Designer does to adjust designs based on newly uncovered constraints.

UX assurance (also known as design review) often takes the form of a formal step in the team's definition of "done" for stories and is the time the Designer spends reviewing development work to ensure that it meets any agreed standards.

HCD Activities and Artifacts

DEVELOPMENT

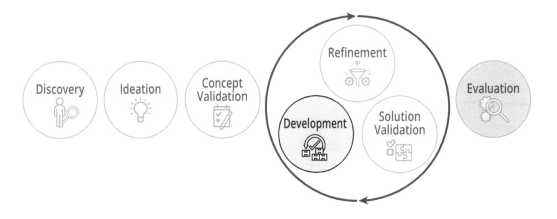

	Research *Participation in agile events*	**Design** In-flight decision support UX assurance (design review)
Example Artifacts	**Research** *None*	**Design** Style guide and pattern library updates
Purpose/Activity	Releasable products, produced as expected In-flight decisions/adjustments that reflect design intent	

Figure 4.2   HCD activities and artifacts in development.

Design Artifacts of Development

Updates to style guides or pattern libraries—if in-flight design support creates a new design pattern, the Designer should update the relevant documentation.

HCD and Solution Validation

During solution validation, the team ensures that the solution they are building meets the "done right" criteria for release. The team does solution validation at a higher level of fidelity than previous concept validation efforts. This may be a model or prototype that more closely resembles the product that will be built, or it may be the actual product as it is being built. In either case, the team is looking to ensure that users understand and can successfully use the solution that will be delivered. Solution validation is a prelaunch activity, which means that the research is conducted ahead of the full release of the product or feature, so decisions can be made in time for the planned release.

From a team standpoint, solution validation leads to two key outcomes (see also Figure 4.3):

HCD Activities and Artifacts

SOLUTION VALIDATION

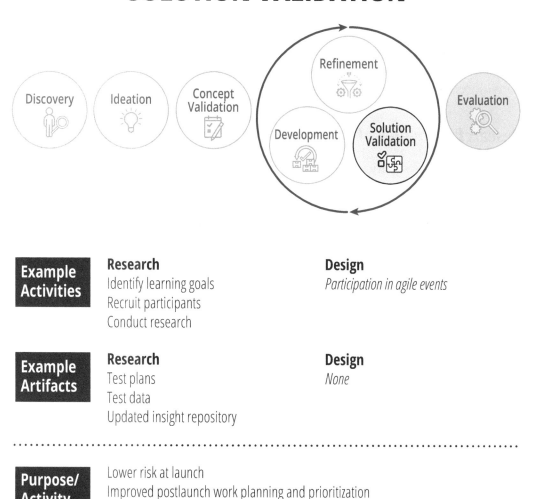

Example Activities	**Research** Identify learning goals Recruit participants Conduct research	**Design** *Participation in agile events*
Example Artifacts	**Research** Test plans Test data Updated insight repository	**Design** *None*

Purpose/ Activity	Lower risk at launch Improved postlaunch work planning and prioritization	

Figure 4.3   **HCD activities and artifacts in solution validation.**

- Lower risk at launch
- Improved postlaunch work planning and prioritization

Lower Risk at Launch

Solution validation tests a high-fidelity product with actual users. In doing so, the team is able to identify any points of confusion or frustration within the experience and address any red flags before the product reaches its widest audience. This reduces the risk of alienating users or costly support while problems get remediated.

Improved Postlaunch Work Planning and Prioritization

In addition to "red flag" issues that need to be resolved prior to launch, solution validation can reveal smaller issues or opportunities to optimize the experience. It is very common for teams to develop a backlog of "fast follow" work to address known issues that are not considered critical.

Research Activities of Solution Validation

The activities of solution validation are very similar to those described in concept validation, including identifying the team's learning goals, recruiting participants, conducting the research, and sharing findings. The primary difference is that the research is conducted using higher-fidelity products. The most common solution validation research is task completion testing, although other tests can be used to validate specific parts of the experience. For example, a team might do paraphrase testing to ensure that specific copy provides good orientation or decision support.

Research Artifacts of Solution Validation

Just as with activities, the artifacts of solution validation are similar to the artifacts of concept validation, including artifacts used for planning (test plans and test scripts), and the artifacts of the research itself (insights and reporting documentation).

THINK LIKE AN EXPERIENCE DESIGNER

When designing an experience, whether simple or complex, it is helpful to identify and validate not just the experience as a whole, but specific elements of the experience. There are a few concepts used in this book that may be helpful for teams that are reviewing designs with a critical eye.

Awareness: How is the user made aware of your product or service, prior to arrival? How do they know to get here, and what expectations are they arriving with?

Arrival: How long does it take to identify the purpose of your product when a user arrives? For digital products, are you creating an impression using visuals and copy that matches?

Wayfinding: Are a user's first steps obvious? If they are seeking specific activities or information, is that path clear enough for them to find it?

Orientation: Once the user has arrived at the place where they are going to get the required information or take some kind of action, is it easy to understand where they are and what is available to them?

Decision Support: Can you give the user any extra information that will help them in places where they need to make decisions? How can you give them contextual support in the places where they are making choices on what to do next?

Action: Are your calls to action clear and easily findable? Have you identified clear primary actions where possible and given them extra prominence?

Expectation Setting: Once a user has engaged with you in some way, do they leave with a clear understanding of what happens next and how long any follow-up steps take?

Consider a library. A person new to a town might only have the awareness that most towns have a library, have a general sense of what a library should do, and have found basic information (such as hours and location) online. That is a different level of awareness and will bring different expectations than someone who has seen a flyer for a reading that is taking place at the library will have.

Upon arrival, the person new to the community might notice that in addition to books, there are computer stations, a periodicals area, posters indicating family and themed events, and a food donation collection area. Their impression is that the library is not just a "books place" but is instead a "community activity and support" place. From there, this person might get wayfinding help if they are seeking a specific book, while the person looking for a reading will also need their own way wayfinding. For a book reading, the orientation may include information like what the seating options are, how long the reading will be, whether the author will take questions or sign books, and what to do if there is a fire alarm. Someone just looking for a good read might see decision support in the form of staff picks or groupings of book award winners, and they also might need to know how long they can have a book checked out before deciding to borrow it. Just as anywhere else, a clear path to action (finding the checkout desk) is critical for success and a receipt that contains a due date for return and an indication of late fees would set an expectation of what happens next.

To be clear, these ideas interact and overlap, and are not always linear. One library patron might engage in multiple wayfinding and orientation activities as they seek to get a book, use a computer, and attend a reading. Knowing that a reading will take 90 minutes is good orientation, *and* it may affect whether someone decides to stay. The library's "Young Adult Fiction" section serves as wayfinding *and* decision support ("Is this book appropriate for my seventh grader?"). As concepts, these are simply guidelines for understanding different parts of an experience you might want to pay attention to.

HCD and Evaluation

During evaluation, the team ensures that what they have built is useful in the real world. There are a number of methods the team has to do this. In addition to methods incorporating qualitative techniques of previous stages (such as interviews and usability tests), the team can now observe users working with their solutions in the context of actual use. Additionally, teams can incorporate a quantitative gathering of information (such as analytics, surveys, and ratings tools, such as Net Promoter Score (NPS) that reflect large-scale behavior patterns.

The results of both post-release quantitative and qualitative evaluations are brought into subsequent iteration planning and backlog refinement. Frequently, this insight will generate new features and stories for development.

From a team standpoint, evaluation leads to three key outcomes (see also Figure 4.4):

■ Identifying unforeseen issues
■ Identification and prioritization of improvements
■ Product-level success measurement

Identifying Unforeseen Issues

Both quantitative and qualitative evaluation activities are critical because products (and users) in the wild always perform at least a little differently than expected when they were validated in a controlled environment.

HCD Activities and Artifacts

EVALUATION

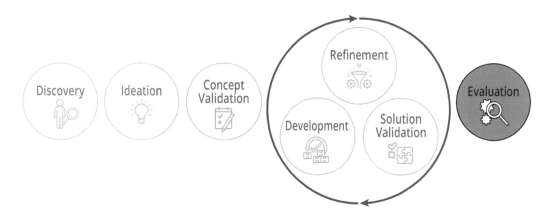

Example Activities	**Research** Contextual inquiry Surveys Interviews Indirect sentiment gathering Digital ethnography Analytics review	**Design** *Participation in agile events*
Example Artifacts	**Research** Sentiment analysis reports Updated insight repository	**Design** *None*

....

Purpose/ Activity	Identify unforeseen issues Identification and prioritization of improvements Product-level success measurement

Figure 4.4   HCD activities and artifacts in evaluation.

Identification and Prioritization of Improvements

In addition to measuring how well a solution is doing, evaluation efforts surface unmet user needs and ideas for how to solve them. It is natural for users that are experiencing a problem or even simply having a suboptimal experience to make suggestions on where the product should go next. The frequency and urgency of suggested improvements provide a great first step for teams deciding what to do next.

Product-Level Success Measurement

HCD practitioners turn feature-level evaluation into a holistic solution-level evaluation. Solution satisfaction is rarely the sum of that solution's parts, which is especially true when considering the qualitative and emotional impact that can lead to solution adoption and loyalty, on one hand, or frustration and abandonment, on the other. It is key that quantitative and qualitative evaluation go hand in hand. Quantitative measures give teams the behavioral "what" while qualitative measures, by contrast, provide the "why."

Research Activities of Evaluation

Contextual inquiry refers to observing a solution being used in its natural context. Unlike usability tests in a controlled environment, this gives the team clearer visibility into user motivations and their attitudes toward the product. The team also gets to see the context within which the user is acting, including things like distractions and concurrent or competing tasks.

Surveys are practically ubiquitous at this point and provide an opportunity for teams to gather information from a wide set of users quickly. They can be particularly valuable for longitudinal feedback understanding how user attitudes change over time as both the product and the landscape of comparable product changes.

Indirect sentiment gathering refers to remote, asynchronous ways to investigate how users are feeling about a product or experience. There are familiar tools that ask users to report directly after their experience. There are more advanced tools and methods that seek to aggregate sentiments from other pools of information, such as:

- Help desk/support tickets
- Community discussion boards
- Social media mentions and activity

The goal of gathering sentiment indirectly is to understand what people say about the product in a variety of contexts, not just during planned research activities. One advantage of looking outside of direct channels like this is that it removes any participation bias (participants often have a desire to either please or be helpful; people calling a help desk or engaging on a discussion board do not). Gathering sentiment from these contexts can reveal different concerns or problems than are stated to researchers.

Digital Ethnography (Community Immersion)

Ethnography is the participant observation of culture. In HCA and software development, it will usually refer to immersive methods of understanding communities by examining their digital footprint (as more literally immersive techniques are cumbersome if even available). This can be done by reviewing their online community behaviors (such as in discussion forums or across social media) where the observation can occur without being intrusive.

Analytics Review

Analytics review is, as it sounds, a review of tracked user behaviors. This allows teams to identify potential difficulties users are having and which may need further qualitative investigation.

Research Artifacts of Evaluation

Research artifacts from a contextual inquiry will resemble the artifacts of previously discussed research efforts from concept and solution validation.

Sentiment analysis reports are the synthesis of any sentiment gathering that the team conducts (such as surveys, etc.) into a report. When sentiment is gathered from sources like surveys or help desk logs, then user comments are often additionally analyzed for key words or other nonnumeric indicators of sentiment.

Note that the data pools from which sentiment is being drawn may contain biases. For example, one might expect a different sentiment from solicited opinions through a survey (polar response) than support calls, which may reflect tool frustration or feelings about the support process itself rather than the product and may also be different than surveys.

HOW MUCH AND WHEN? PLANNING AND EXECUTING HCD WITHIN AGILE

Chapter 5

Bringing Human-Centered Design into Agile

Project management, at its heart, is about *risk* management. Traditional project delivery methods rely on a "waterfall" approach to managing project risks. The phases in this process are usually analysis, requirements gathering, design, construction, testing, and deployment (or something similar). The thinking is that by conducting a review before each stage, project managers can minimize risk simply by ensuring that work on the next phase does not begin until work on the previous phase is completed. This is more difficult than it sounds, however. How can they know if the work is really complete?

In waterfall, design happened in specific and sometimes lengthy stages. A "requirements gathering" stage meant talking to stakeholders to hear what they wanted and then creating a large list of needs and a design stage to create a solution that somehow accomplished all those needs.

Using this approach, risk accumulates because assumptions made in each phase of the traditional project are never tested or validated with users and are, instead, merely vetted internally among the business analysts and subject-matter experts on the team. Because one stage needs to be completed before the next starts, the analysis and design phases can take a year (or more!) to fully document every nuanced detail of the product to be delivered. At that point, the output of these phases is not only stale but also untested and unvalidated by actual users. The result is a "big bang" release where all the functionality developed is released to users all at once. This increases the risk of releasing a product that doesn't offer all the features

DOI: 10.4324/9781003188520-8

and functionality the users desire. It also increases the risk of a complete launch failure for technical reasons.

"Waterfall" Delivery and Its Challenges

Poor customer experience is not the only risk of waterfall. There are additional concerns specific to the implementation and delivery of working software at a large enough scale.

Even with a comprehensive set of requirements, issues can arise during the implementation stage of waterfall releases, especially for large efforts. One major problem is that, even with all the time spent, technical assumptions are often wrong. The people generating the requirements either don't have a deep enough knowledge of user needs or the time to work through the details or perfect foresight about specific aspects. Bad assumptions can also occur through no fault of the team. Because the requirements definition process can take so long, technology advances can mean that the design was created using one set of constraints while delivery is being accomplished with different constraints.

To further complicate things, technical problems typically arise during code integration. Big ones. Because code from the various teams is not integrated and tested as a unit until the end of the project, broken builds and costly rework become the norm. Source control systems in waterfall development tend to contain multiple branches, requiring painstaking merging at the end of the project, a process that almost always results in something breaking. Bugs in this process are notoriously difficult to identify and fixing them can be a nightmare. Recriminations between developers, analysts, and testers about who is to blame become commonplace, and if the code eventually does get integrated, major schedule slippage is the most likely result.

At this point, testing on the newly integrated codebase begins, often ending tragically with multiple errors that require a coordinated effort by teams to resolve. These are generally not small issues but showstopping flaws forcing reanalysis along with major redesign and rework. Not infrequently, entire features need to be de-scoped because the team knows they can never make them work in the remaining time. It is during this period that teams realize that what they designed and constructed doesn't quite solve the problem at hand or did so in a suboptimal way. Figure 5.1 shows how risk accumulates and value delivery is deferred on a waterfall project.

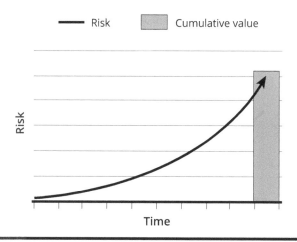

Figure 5.1   Risk and value delivery on a waterfall project.

Replacing Waterfall with Agile

With all the risks of waterfall, it was not uncommon for huge, expensive efforts to fail altogether. Agile development emerged to mitigate these risks with an improved way for knowledge workers to collaborate. In Agile development, cross-functional teams are formed with the goal of understanding user needs and then testing solutions by delivering small batches of value rapidly and getting user feedback before iteratively and incrementally enhancing the solution.

Agile product development represents a clear shift in mentality that is more focused on the customer and providing end-user value quickly than on extensive planning and documentation. Agile never supposes that there is a comprehensive "requirements" document at the beginning of the project because experience has shown that creating such a document at that point is simply not possible. Instead, the Agile approach tests assumptions by delivering a small unit of value to the end user, learning from it, then iterating based on that learning.

Agile is especially effective in software development, but this mindset and approach can be used successfully for any type of knowledge work, which is defined as any work in which the workers know more about the subject than their managers.[1] Agile frameworks like Scrum and XP explicitly support the Agile mindset that gives teams of knowledge workers the "permission"

---

[1] Peter Drucker, 1967, *The Effective Executive*, Harper & Row Publishers

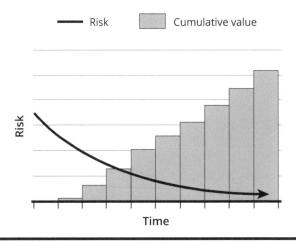

Figure 5.2   Risk is mitigated and value delivered early in Agile projects. The bars here represent cumulative value delivery.

to experiment and the tools to ensure that learning from their experiments is channeled into future endeavors.

HCD shares an important philosophical foundation with Agile, upon which all integration of the two approaches will rest: It is best to learn about product and delivery efforts in the simplest, fastest, and cheapest way possible. Figure 5.2 shows how risk is mitigated by small increments of early value delivery in an Agile project.

Organic Overlaps between Agile and HCD

Agilists are familiar with the "fail fast, fail often" approach. In Agile, it is considered a good thing for a team to spend a small amount of time developing a solution that fails so they can quickly pivot to testing an alternate solution. The very idea is to slice product delivery into small enough pieces that problems with the team's underlying assumptions can be tested quickly, issues that show up in development can be identified and fixed, and the learning can happen in a way that doesn't jeopardize entire product launches. A certain amount of rework (called refactoring by Agilists) is accepted in the name of delivering quickly and taking in real feedback rather than being able to see around every possible corner.

HCD is a practice built around avoiding many of the same risks, although sometimes at different stages of delivery, and addressing additional common risks as well.

- By identifying and validating user needs, Agile teams mitigate the risk of spending time building things that users don't actually need or want. Chasing unnecessary features is an incredibly expensive proposition.
- By validating designs with the users of their products at key points, Agile teams minimize rework based on unsuccessful design approaches or poor assumptions.
- By evaluating products after they are delivered, Agile teams ensure that their investment in further product improvement is well targeted.

Even without formally incorporating Human-Centered Design (HCD), Agile classically already integrates *some* HCD as part of its approach. In the cycle of build > evaluate > iterate, the evaluation stage is where all HCD takes place. That is to say, even if there is no engagement with users in discovery or ideation, there is an expectation that user feedback is gathered when products are released and that this feedback provides a team with improvements. In a sense, the evaluation stage stands in for discovery (users will now tell teams if they are solving a problem they don't have), concept validation (users will tell teams if something was a bad idea), and solution validation (users will tell teams if there are specific places where they are having problems).

For certain kinds of projects, the evaluation phase can be enough to keep the team moving in a good direction.

Here are two prime examples of this.

1. **The very beginning stages of a new product or feature, iterated rapidly**

   The easiest way to locate the overlaps between Agile and HCD is by considering what can happen when new projects or features get spun up. Often, an idea is expressed as one or two important things that need to happen then developed very quickly and shown to a handful of key people to get feedback and iterate. When they represent users and stakeholders, this takes the place of user outreach steps. This typically happens with a small team, where each iteration has low-enough stakes that the team can safely follow the feedback they get. Once a product has a high-enough profile or a large-enough team, however, this approach tends to become risky or inadequate.

2. **A very mature product with an expected sunset**

   Occasionally, products live in a state where only small changes are required, usually based on ongoing feedback. This is the case when most strategic decisions have already been baked in and only small refinements are necessary for the remaining life cycle of the product.

Where Does HCD Fit in Agile?

When teams and organizations transition from waterfall to Agile, figuring out how design fits into the new delivery method can become confusing. Waterfall's defined steps (requirements gathering and design, etc.) give teams time to complete the discovery and ideation phases. In Agile, it can be considerably less clear where these steps fit into the picture.

It is important to understand from the outset that these activities do not go into a single, neat, linear place when integrating Agile with HCD. However, *this does not mean that they don't take place*. Instead, it means that each step is adaptive to the team's ongoing activities. Just as there is no one exactly right way to implement Agile, there is no one-size-fits-all way to integrate Agile and HCD.

Specifically, when and how design steps occur is going to depend on:

■ The size of the product
■ The scale of the team/organization and the amount of interdependency between teams
■ The stakes of the release (more on this later)

Why Not Use HCD "Instead" of Agile?

If teams can get information about what to make from end users using HCD methods at the outset, why use Agile at all? Why not just build what users have asked for and assume this will be successful? The answer is that neither users nor product teams are infallible. It is simply impossible to know that the team has built a good solution without getting user feedback, and there will always be ways to make it better. Agile provides the framework and mindset to do exactly that. Human-Centered Agile provides an improved "anything" from the very first iteration because of its constant stakeholder inclusion.

How HCD Applies to the Agile Mindset

HCD work is directed at the questions of "right problem" and "right solution" in addition to evaluating built products ("done right"). HCD is interested in understanding users' attitudes, behaviors, and expectations to better inform development work. Development work, by nature, is confined to one solution, delivered as instructed (which is a different, but important, perspective on "done right"). This happens throughout the delivery life cycle, not just at a few specific moments.

Agilists often consider the Product Owner the first voice of the customer in deciding what to build, release, and iterate upon. Then, some form of post-release evaluation and feedback provides the second voice of the customer. Table 5.1 shows what team activity looks like in each of the design phases when using traditional Agile processes (without incorporating HCD practices) compared with Human-Centered Agile.

Table 5.1 A Side-by-Side Comparison of Agile without and with HCD

	Traditional Agile without HCD	*Human-Centered Agile*
Discovery	Teams receive user needs and desires based on the Product Owner's interpretation, which is typically a mix of business needs and limited direct user feedback.	Teams learn and/or proactively validate user needs and desires, seeking to understand specific attitudes and behaviors toward their proposed product vision or product updates. At the same time, business needs are elicited from the Product Owner and other business stakeholders.
Ideation	Teams work on whatever the Product Owner requests. Technical feasibility and comfort are the most significant constraints on product design. Often, only one solution is considered.	Teams use their learnings from discovery to conduct collaborative ideation with the Product Owner and other team members, including business analysts, developers, HCD practitioners, and possibly even users, to generate and compare multiple concepts.
Concept Validation	Teams assume that their solution is valuable and that it can be iterated upon after release.	Teams subject their solution concepts to feedback from users for validation, to support a pivot-or-persevere decision at an early stage in the process.

(Continued)

Table 5.1 (Continued)

	Traditional Agile without HCD	*Human-Centered Agile*
Refinement	The Product Owner and team update stories based on technical constraints. The Product Owner provides additional guidance as required for development.	Teams apply insights from validation to solution development. HCD practitioners are engaged in story refinement to ensure that the development reflects the intended solution and is grounded in user needs and expectations.
Development	Changes made based on new needs or unforeseen constraints are made by developers and favor expedience.	Developed product is reviewed for UX assurance. Changes made based on new needs or unforeseen constraints are made collaboratively by developers and Designers and weighing trade-offs between expedience and experience.
Solution Validation	Teams assume that their solution will be generally correct, and any emergent issues can be resolved through iteration after release.	Teams put solutions (or prototypes in varying degrees of fidelity) in front of end users to ensure that the product is understood and serves needs as expected prior to release.
Evaluation	Teams incorporate whatever live feedback and insight is gathered from actual users following a launch into the next product cycle. This is typically obtained using high-level product success metrics, broadly applied satisfaction results, or helpdesk/support issue reports.	Teams include user-based measurement of the postlaunch success of their product and prioritize any gaps or additional features based on feedback.

When incorporating HCD, teams transition to a process that involves users of their end product in as many of the five stages as possible.

Engaging users throughout the entire process improves every step of the product life cycle by reducing the risk of misfiring and delivering products that don't actually meet user needs. From initial concepts all the way through implementation, users are key stakeholders, and teams should seek their input. In the early steps, they help teams ensure that they are solving the right problems. In the later steps, they help teams build the right solutions effectively.

The "Experimenting" Mindset

Experiments help teams and leaders embrace uncertainty. Incorporating experiments as a practice is a clear way to signal that there is value in admitting what isn't known while making an effort to address knowledge gaps. It also provides an opportunity for teams to improve their products and processes.

At the team level, experimenting comes pretty naturally. The experiment is meant to answer a specific question with a clear hypothesis. For example, "A bigger button will get clicked more often." An experiment is one specific research approach, and an approachable way to infuse some research, but it is not the only one.

Where Do Experiments Come From?

At a product level, experiments are born from a team's desire to learn the approach to solving the problem that is preferred by their users. This takes the form of opportunities to make hypotheses about what users might want and test those hypotheses. This can happen in discovery, in the form of gathering information from users, and from ideation efforts that produce solution concepts (such as lightweight prototypes) that are presented to users. In both cases, these are treated as experiments with specific learning goals, and teams have permission to both validate and invalidate their assumptions, as well as the opportunity to make decisions about how to proceed. In this way, the learning that results from these experiments informs delivery by helping teams understand user attitudes about what constitutes the right solution and done right.

At a process level, an experiment might emerge from a team's retrospective in the form of a new working agreement to be tried for a sprint or two "just to see if it works better this way." Similarly, experiments can emerge from program-level retrospectives, which have a different structure and focus than team retrospectives but still provide insights into program-level behaviors and opportunities for improvement.

How Are Experiments Conducted?

Supporting the change to an experimental mindset requires soliciting experiment ideas across the program. These ideas can come from teams wanting support for a particular experiment, program-level meetings where individuals propose experiments to address concerns or knowledge gaps, or even channels, like a suggestion box or "wall of suggestions," that allow individuals to propose ideas asynchronously and anonymously. Once experiments are identified, it is important they be tracked in such a way that the results are available to the team later to inform future activities.

It is crucial to ensure that experiments, their progress, and their outcomes are visible to all, not just a few people. Additionally, failed experiments should be celebrated—with a true experimental mindset, teams will have some "failures" (overturned assumptions) alongside their "successes" (validated assumptions). In fact, failure is a misleading word, because as long as the experiment resulted in learning, it didn't fail. By highlighting this frequently and focusing on the good that came from the experiments instead of the fact that they "failed," leadership can demonstrate support for their teams and this new way of working and thinking.

Programs should highlight experiments, and their results, within the program. Doing this sustains the spirit of innovation and experimentation by periodically showcasing decisions and innovations one team has guided through their experiments.

Iterations, Not Just Increments

One outcome of experiments (and, in fact, all research) is iteration. It is surprising how often teams and programs do not understand the difference between iterations and increments, which is similar to the difference between a painting (iterative) and a jigsaw puzzle (incremental).

In a jigsaw puzzle, one piece after another is added until it is done. The people building it never go back and improve a puzzle piece or group of pieces. It is an *assembly* process, not an *improvement* process.

A painting tends to work the opposite way. The painters start with sketches and basic composition, refining along the way. They may refine in different stages, but every area of the painting is reworked more than once. The painters step back, evaluate their work, and iterate until the lighting, shading, and texture are done.

It is essential for any Agile teams (perhaps especially *Human-Centered* Agile teams) to iterate. Teams that don't iterate don't innovate. Teams building products incrementally, not iteratively, is an all-too-common anti-pattern. The whole point of building work in small batches is to get fast and frequent feedback from users on it. The whole point of that feedback is to improve future deliveries. Teams who don't receive feedback or use it to improve their product are often applying an Agile veneer to a waterfall process. Don't do that.

"Build and See" Agile to "Stakes-based" Human-Centered Agile

Shifting from "build it and see" to stakes-based thinking is a critical step in moving toward Human-Centered Agile because that thinking allows teams to match the level of time, money, and effort spent on HCD research to the stakes of the feature or product. This shift encourages early discussions about the stakes of features and which risks can be mitigated by better understanding users or through direct observation of user interactions with proposed features. It also emphasizes measuring outcomes consistently.

THE TOOLS TO DISPROVE THE HYPOTHESIS

No matter how well constructed a problem definition is, there is always the possibility that the intended solution does not perform as expected. Regardless of whether a solution was devised by a C-suite Executive or teams on the ground, sometimes outcomes stymie expectations.

It's essential for teams to learn and adjust as quickly (and, therefore cheaply) as possible, even when what they learn is not aligned to the expectations of leadership. This is one of the common friction points of Agile. Leadership sometimes needs to be coaxed to accept evidence that goes against their initial vision. This is an important part of any Agile framework and a nonnegotiable part of Human-Centered Agile.

As Jeff Gothelf put it during the 24 Hours of UX conference in June 2021:

> The techniques [UX practitioners] practice provide the evidence that the outcome is contradicting the plan.

If an organization is not set up to respond to new information and adjust and is, instead, directed to adhere to the leadership-provided plan, then we must question whether they have genuinely adopted an Agile mindset or are simply using some Agile practices to deliver predetermined software in a slightly more efficient way.

Human-Centered Agile Empowers Teams

Product Owners own and prioritize the backlog on Agile teams, and this is true in Human-Centered Agile as well. The difference is how teams get information about user needs, insights, and preferences. In Human-Centered Agile, the team no longer relies on the Product Owner as a proxy for the user. Instead, they have access to the aggregated, organized, and analyzed sentiment from dozens, hundreds, or sometimes thousands of users. That insight helps the team write better stories, select better design options, enhance their acceptance criteria, and inform backlog prioritization and refinement.

Embracing Uncertainty

One of the difficult parts about moving toward Agile and product thinking is the idea that teams don't necessarily "know" what their final product is going to be when they begin. That generates two different kinds of uncertainty:

- Product uncertainty
- Delivery uncertainty

Accepting both types of uncertainty requires an additional shift toward a willingness to see overall strategy as flexible and responsive to new information.

IF EMBRACING UNCERTAINTY IS SO SIMPLE, WHY DOESN'T IT HAPPEN?

Before talking about making the shift to uncertainty, it's worth discussing what is so appealing about predictability.

There's an old story about a man searching for something under a streetlight. A stranger walks up and asks the man what he is looking for. He replies that he's lost his keys, so they both look under the streetlight together. After a few minutes, the stranger asks if the man is sure he lost them here, and the man discloses that he actually lost them in the park. The stranger then asks why he is searching here, and the man says, "This is where the light is."

When setting a budget or evaluating a manager, being able to make predictions about what the work will cost and how long it will take is *very* useful. Teams can make easier strategic decisions when they know the cost of their efforts up front and more easily plan associated activities (such as sales, marketing, and communications efforts) if they know exactly what will be delivered.

The problem is that, for all the (supposed) "light" provided by all this preplanning work, the *value* may be in the "park" instead. Predictability is important but not more so than the actual value delivered. Often, acting as if predictability trumps value delivery means that "sticking to the plan" becomes the primary mindset rather than "learning and adjusting." The goal is to be a team or program that becomes resilient to the necessary changes that inevitably arise, not to stick to the plan.

This goal requires a new way of thinking as well as a new approach. A team should be comfortable with a process, like

> We know what we want to accomplish but we aren't sure what the solution looks like. When we come up with ideas, we talk them through and size them, then pull them based on expected value rather than trying to know the requirements up front. When estimates change, we reassess.

Product Uncertainty

Teams used to working with traditional methods often start with a list of requirements as thick as a telephone book. These teams typically feel great comfort in this requirements document because, if they are building what was in that list, they are "on the right track." Except when they aren't, which frequently turns out to be the case. Usually, teams don't learn this until the end of the project, at which time change orders are issued, increasing costs and exceeding budgets. It then becomes necessary to find someone to blame.

Agile and product thinking believe that a "correct" requirements document at the beginning of the project offers a false sense of security. No professional using traditional methods, in any field, has ever had a Gantt chart look the same at the end of a major project as it did in the beginning. That's because things change, and Agile helps teams embrace that change.

Agile helps focus on value, the outcomes a team hopes to achieve with their work. By focusing on and gauging delivery on the value rather than percent complete, teams can reduce their stress levels by allowing themselves to experiment. Once this occurs, they are free to challenge the assumptions they've made and try innovative new solutions, knowing that not all their experiments will be successful, which is OK. To support this change teams should

- identify the outcomes delivered by each feature and be explicit about how success is to be measured.
- make sure teams are aware that their success is determined primarily by how well the product does, not by how quickly something is delivered.
- create actual measurement meetings on an agreed-on cadence.

Delivery Uncertainty

Along with shifting to an outcome-driven approach with problem-solving, teams and programs need to embrace the idea that initially, they may not know how long something will take to accomplish. Their sense of effort and progress will get clearer as they go. Agile has tools to handle this, where initial estimates are seen as less reliable than later ones and teams are allowed to refine and resize work as their assumptions get proved or disproved. However, it's not enough to say, "That's just how Agile works," and then trust that delivery uncertainty will be accepted. Many programs often fail to make the mindset shift that allows Agile teams to succeed. To support this change teams should

- make sure they understand that sizing is an iterative process, subject to change as features and stories are refined.
- regularly incorporate activities that identify and discuss risks. After all, a desire for waterfall-like delivery predictability rests on the idea that it's possible to know everything crucial right up front. Discussions about risk, by their nature, invite understanding that this is not actually true.

Chapter 6

"What Are the Stakes?"

The goal of a product team's research is to limit the risk and expense of solving the wrong problems or building solutions in ways that are not successful for the user. This risk affects more than just development costs, reaching into product reputation and customer confidence. With that in mind, teams should ask, "What are the consequences if our assumptions happen to be wrong?" Or, more succinctly, "What are the stakes of this research?" It is this question that drives which research is necessary and how research gets prioritized.

Product Release Stakes

Suppose a team is planning to spend a few hours building a small story and has little reason to think that adding the story would be harmful to the customer's experience. The team may decide to forgo any research for it. After all, why spend ten times as many hours doing research than actually developing the story? In this case, the best path might be to build functionality and iterate after getting user feedback. By contrast, stories and larger units of work, like features, that are expensive to build or likely to have a large impact on user behavior merit more research.

While lower stakes features are less likely to require research, it is worth noting that a large cluster of small features can amount to both a large shift in overall user experience and represent a volume of total development time and large enough to elevate it to a level that requires validation testing with users.

DOI: 10.4324/9781003188520-9

The Factors of Stakes-Based Decision-Making

If the question is, "What are the consequences if our assumptions happen to be wrong?" the answer can have a few different forms, some more obvious than others. When considering what the stakes are of conducting or forego-ing research, consider the following factors.

Level of Effort

This is the first and most obvious factor in the stakes. Production quality code is expensive to create. How much time and money are about to be put into making something that the team thinks users want? What if they don't?

Support Costs

Like delivery costs, this is a direct financial cost. Releasing confusing soft-ware leads to additional costs in the form of help desk support and commu-nications. This is a case in which "measure twice, cut once" can save some real headaches for other teams that support the product.

Audience Size

How large is the audience that will be impacted by the release? The stakes are low if the team and a few friendly stakeholders are the first users. If they mess up, the team will work through it, and everyone will accept the mis-steps as progress. If there are a million users, even a small misstep can cre-ate confusion (again, support requests) or dissatisfaction.

It's worth noting that seeking qualitative user feedback is only *one* of the tools to reduce the stakes of a wide release. Teams will often engage in fea-ture pilots, such as in A/B or multivariate testing, that allow a small subset of features to become available to a limited audience.

Communications Investment and Audience Expectations

What kind of effort has been spent to generate awareness and enthusi-asm for the release? Is it an anticipated launch or update? Have audience expectations been raised through marketing or other communications? If the feature is high profile, the potential negative impact of releas-ing a disappointing product may be higher than the cost of develop-ing it. This is important because not every user will give a product a second chance, a very real adoption risk to releasing a highly touted but poor-performing product.

Centrality of Experience

Game Designers use the concept of a "core loop" to describe what is central to the experience.

> *The core loop is essentially the very heartbeat of your game. It is a series or chain of actions that is repeated over and over as the primary flow of your players' experience. It's the core essence of why we return to play games over and over again.*

> **— Kevin Wolstenholme**

This concept is applicable to many products—is the team changing something that is central to the experience they are providing, and that is part of the reason a customer returns? A team working on an online shopping site that changes the checkout interaction is changing something more central to the experience than a team that is updating a "buy it again" reminder feature. This does not mean that the experience is unimportant, just that the immediate impact of the change to users is lower, possibly allowing for better postlaunch problem-solving. If the team is updating a central part of the experience, that should be a factor as teams evaluate the research stakes—releases that change primary experiences contain an elevated risk if the update isn't useful or detracts from the experience.

Reputation

Independent of immediate costs of user acceptance of the product is the risk that releases that are not useful or confusing can, over time, degrade both the quality of the experience and the product's (and perhaps the brand's) reputation among users and potential users. When thinking about reputation as part of determining the stakes, teams should consider how often they are doing evaluative work in general, not just for a specific release.

Morale Costs

The costs of releasing a poor product that come to mind are usually the costs of building and supporting the software itself or building and maintaining a user base. However, there is an additional risk worth considering when evaluating the stakes of a release: team morale. Members of teams who repeatedly feel like they are unable to release products that deliver value tend to look for more fulfilling opportunities.

Stakes per Life-Cycle Stage

Discovery

If teams have not uncovered their users' needs, they risk building something that is simply unwanted, which can be an expensive undertaking. Additionally, if teams build many unwanted features, these may crowd the experience that was desired. More features do not always mean more success. In fact, "feature cramming" is a known product risk. Sometimes, not building an unnecessary feature really is the best decision. It also happens to be the cheapest one, mapping to the Agile Manifesto principle "Simplicity—the art of maximizing the amount of work not done—is essential."[1]

Ideation and Concept Validation

Whether emerging from ideation with competing concepts or hoping to move forward with one particular concept, the outcome of concept validation is a pivot-or-persevere decision—a team is trying to decide whether to move forward with a given solution. In a sense, the stakes are the cost of refining, building, and supporting the product. If the team has validated a problem only to latch onto the first solution that comes to mind or the most technically expedient solution without comparing alternatives, they risk generating solutions that are more complex or costly than necessary or are simply not as useful in solving the problem as the users want them to be.

Solution Validation

Solution validation can be the difference between releasing a product with major issues and support costs or releasing a product that performs well. Unnoticed issues can become costly in terms of users either rejecting the solution entirely or needing expensive technical support. Solution validation should

---

[1] https://agilemanifesto.org/principles.fhtml

not be limited to functional testing and technical success—a poor or confusing experience can be as much a problem for users as a broken piece of functionality. Testing prior to release mitigates the risk of going live with "red flag" issues and that users are disappointed or frustrated with their experience.

Evaluation

Understanding the health of the product is critical for determining and prioritizing future efforts. If the product is not performing well and the team is not evaluating it, this can have an ongoing impact on the product's successful adoption and ongoing level of engagement from users, and future improvements will not be prioritized based on what audiences want or need. In considering the stakes of evaluation, teams should ask how they are determining whether their product is succeeding.

Stakes per Specific Decisions

Often, when teams first start taking on research as part of their delivery process, it can become tempting to frame every single design decision as something that requires a specific research effort. Which shade of blue? Should the call to action (CTA) be a circle, oval, or rounded rectangle? Should it have a 12- or 14-point font? Which typeface?

Design is something that everyone has an opinion on. Often, there aren't simple, objective measurements for these types of granular questions, especially during ideation. Teams can refer to best design practices appropriate to their solution and occasionally find research backing up specific design decisions, but while some usage patterns are observable and backed by research, teams will need to make many decisions using their own hypotheses and best judgments about what works best.

It is possible to test granular decisions down to the micro level. There are tools for that kind of research, and there are definitely occasions for which testing granular details is warranted, but most decisions do not fall into this category for the vast majority of teams and products.

Teams typically seek to answer more basic questions, such as:

■ "Does the user notice that this button exists, or did they hunt for it?"
■ "Did the user have clear expectations of what happens when they press these links or buttons?"
■ "Can users find what they need and complete their tasks?"

Chapter 7

Planning and Conducting HCD Activities in Agile

There is a wide variety of HCD work that takes place before, during, and following development work. Since research has a runway that precedes development work, Product Owners and HCD practitioners must look beyond the current sprint to plan their work.

This earlier life-cycle work can be difficult to keep track of and can be a particular challenge for teams used to thinking of only development work as "the work," thus focusing on more immediate terms. Looking ahead can cause friction between the HCD and Agile mindsets, but it shouldn't. This planning does not mean that teams become inflexible (locked into long-term commitments), but it does mean that teams can learn, iterate, and mitigate risks earlier and at lower cost than learning exclusively through building release-quality software.

Using a Research Roadmap

A Research Roadmap helps teams bridge that gap by bringing Agile values and planning into the context of research. For example, by incorporating a Research Roadmap, teams can maintain a flexibility of operations and a clear, shared understanding of goals while also improving their estimation of effort sizes and keeping research fresh and relevant to near-term work without sacrificing the value it brings.

DOI: 10.4324/9781003188520-10

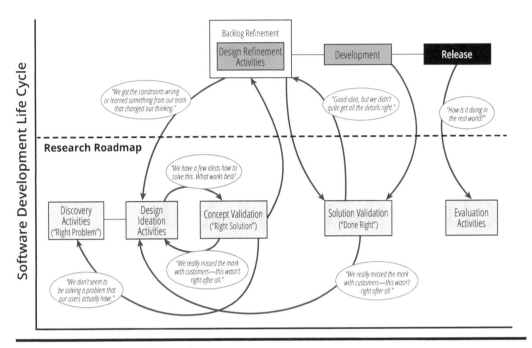

Figure 7.1 The Research Roadmap.

A Research Roadmap (see Figure 7.1) is similar to a product roadmap. Its goal is to give a high-level overview of the upcoming research efforts, including a sense of what overall learning goals they serve and where they fall in terms of timeline and priority. The Research Roadmap runs parallel to the product roadmap, since the two have interdependencies.

Having research in a roadmap view makes it possible to look at the breadth of planned HCD work and prioritize it as a whole set. This also gives a team the ability to look at HCD work per epic and/or feature to see whether critical unknowns are being addressed so that the team is strategically mitigating as much product development risk as possible.

Practitioners will notice two things about this figure: research and design activities are separated and many HCD activities are not consumed in the same sprint.

Research and Design Activities Are Separated

Research and design activities are separated to emphasize that research is an integral part of the Human-Centered Design (HCD) process and highlight the fact that it requires a different sort of work, which is often thought of as part of design. A Designer can make a wireframe with just an idea (or set of requirements) and a computer but cannot make a journey map that way.

Similarly, design activities guided by previous research or best practices are ongoing throughout the process, without requiring further research. Stories are based on the knowledge of the users, but they often get refined based on technical and business constraints or simply new decisions. When those refinements have a front-end impact, the Designer should be involved in the refinement process to make sure the updates reflect the user goals rather than being decisions for expediency.

Many HCD Activities Are Not Consumed in the Current Sprint

Research activities require time for team digestion and response. Obviously, teams wishing to learn or validate what users' needs and desires are cannot do so a week before implementation and still expect time for refinement. Conversely, teams already committed to doing work in an upcoming sprint would fail to see the purpose of doing discovery to impact the current planned release. Any discovery activities at that point would only influence future releases.

The Research Roadmap and Research Strategy

Aligning a Research Roadmap and a product roadmap allows the team to get a clear enough picture of their overall workload to see what products/features are in the pipeline, even if just in general terms. Seeing both gives teams a clear picture of which releases have, or might need, research support.

It is a good practice to review the Research Roadmap directly following a review of the product roadmap so the product research needs are apparent. By seeing where all these features are in their cycle, teams can begin to answer questions, like

- What discovery is still needed?
- Can discovery research support multiple releases?
- What proportion of the team's time is going to be spent on each of the "right problem, right solution, done right" questions?

For example, the team might wish to conduct

- discovery research that is truly exploratory and organized around discovering unmet needs and opportunities.

■ discovery research that is required well ahead of implementation for certain features to ensure the intended feature solves a need for users.
■ collaborative ideation for some features, followed by concept validation of the high-level solutions, so the right solution can be planned.
■ solution validation (usability testing) for products one to three sprints out so findings can be integrated into stories and implementation.
■ evaluation efforts following specific releases.

Linking HCD Stories with the Product Roadmap

In order to use a Research Roadmap, teams need to be able to link research stories to their corresponding efforts on a product roadmap. For early-stage research and design work (discovery through concept validation), this will mean linking to an epic that describes the problem a team is seeking to address. For later work (solution validation or evaluation), these stories can be tied to features. In either case, research work should be identifiable and trackable as part of an effort that is reflected on the product roadmap. This ensures that the team is tracking all research and design activities (i.e., there is no "off the books" work) and that all work has an agreed-on purpose (i.e., there is no "free-floating" work).

Epics, Discovery Work, and "Right Problem"

The research work of problem exploration and problem validation should be attached to a problem-oriented epic on the roadmap, which articulates a problem to be solved.

In Chapter 3, the discussion of epics was focused on covering the following questions:

1. "What is the problem that we are trying to solve for users, and what value do we expect them to receive?"
2. "Is this a problem that needs to be solved?"
3. "What are the 'stakes'"? (See Chapter 6.)
4. "What is the benefit to the business of solving this problem?"
5. "What types of solutions are acceptable to users and feasible to deliver, at a level of effort appropriate to the problem?" In other words, "What types of solutions are acceptable and within reach?"
6. "How might the success of this solution be measured?"

Example Epic

Imagine that a company has been providing support to their customers through phone support during business hours. They have received a handful of requests for 24/7 support, including some very frustrated customers. Before deciding how to best provide additional support, the team is interested in understanding whether this is truly an issue that needs solving for their customers and what expectations customers have regarding support in general.

The epic will contain a problem statement but from a team perspective.

EPIC-001: After-Hours Support

The team believes that there is a significant need for additional support beyond phone-based support during daytime hours and needs to determine how to provide support so that customers feel confident in their relationship with our business.

- Expected outcomes:
- Validate whether there is unmet interest/need in additional support
- Identify user sentiments and expectations about additional support (i.e., what kind of support is acceptable and useful)
- Generate ideas for providing additional support
- Validate and select feature(s) for delivery
- Generate success measurement criteria for selected feature

This will lead to specific research stories. A research user story behaves as any other user story does with slight variation. The story is best written in a "As a team, we want to learn X, so that we can decide Y" fashion, where the decision points are baked in. This prevents research from becoming unfocused in its approach. Notably, it is possible to have more than one research story that shares common learning goals.

For a research story, the definition of ready should include:

- Learning Goals: Hypothesis tested or types of insights expected
- Intended methodology
- Acceptable format of delivery/share-out
- Recruitment approach

In other aspects, which include creating clear acceptance criteria and doing a team-based refinement and story-pointing effort, the story should be treated as any other.

Example Research Stories for Discovery

The following are example research stories that might be tied to the example epic and are intended to fulfill acceptance criteria (ACs) 1 and 2. Because research stories are about gathering evidence, on completion, the team may decide that enough evidence was gathered to make good decisions and that these AC were met or that they may decide that additional evidence is needed that requires additional effort.

Story: As a product team, we want to validate that users are regularly experiencing frustration that their issues cannot be addressed after hours so that we can address their needs in an appropriate way.

Learning goal 1: Identify current user expectation of support. We would like to know whether users are aware that support is only available during limited hours or whether their initial expectation is that they have 24-hour support. Understanding whether there is a gap between expectation and actual experience will help us determine whether to provide further support.

Learning goal 2: Identify the preferred method of support. We will include a question about how they expect and/or would prefer to reach us after hours.

Methodology: 12–15 one-on-one interviews, expected to take 10 minutes or less.

Recruitment: We will be offering a small incentive ($10 account credit) and sending a recruitment email to a sample group of users who have opted in for research participation.

Share-out: There will be a one-page or shorter summary of responses, with an analysis of current support expectations, and preferred support channels/methods.

Story: As a product team, we want to validate that users are regularly experiencing frustration that their issues cannot be addressed after hours so that we can address their needs in an appropriate way.

Learning goal 1: Identify whether users who have recently called customer support experienced "wait frustration" because they were not able to contact us immediately.

Methodology: A onetime brief (no more than 3 questions) multiple-choice survey of customer support users in the past month, with an option for additional comments.

We expect a "polar" response and that frustrated users will be more motivated responders. In this case, this is not a problem—we will evaluate reports of frustration both as a percentage of respondents and as a percentage of survey recipients.

Recruitment: We will be offering a small incentive ($10 account credit) and sending a survey for response to *all* users that have contacted us for customer support in the past 30 days.
Share-out: There will be a one-page or shorter summary of responses.

As with any story, research stories should be reviewed, refined, and estimated with the whole team, who may have questions or additional thoughts about any of the details provided: methodology, questions of interest, or how information is distributed. It will also be up to the team to determine how to capture additional work—for example, the generation of an interview script might become an acceptance criteria item, while the actual conducting of an interview could be a task.

These examples are for problem validation tied to an epic, but this story structure works for any research stories, including concept and solution validation stories.

Ideation and Concept Validation Stories Prior to Features

Like research stories, ideation stories are tied to an epic and precede identification of a specific solution. The goal of an ideation story is to generate solution concepts that can be evaluated relative to one another. In the example provided, if the team validated a need for additional support, there would be a follow-up story to generate solution concepts for providing that support.

Story: As a product team, we want to generate and estimate multiple-solution approaches that solve a user's need for after-hours support so that we can identify the most promising solution candidates to deliver.

AC1: We will conduct a workshop-style ideation session, with the goal of producing 3–5 feasible designs.
AC2: All designs will be given a rough estimate (T-shirt size) for level of effort, a score for feasibility, and a score for expected user desirability.

Upon completion of this story, candidate solution(s) will be selected for either development or for further validation if risks are identified (including feasibility assessment and/or user acceptance)

Note that this team has chosen to collaborate on their ideation, so rather than describe a specific number of designs, they put a target outcome instead. This allows for flexibility in their ideation process. If this team were to produce ideas that seemed promising and wanted to ensure that users would be receptive to their solution(s) before investing in substantial development work, they might then create a new research story for concept validation.

Story: As a product team, we want to understand which proposed after-hours support options users will find most helpful so that we know whether to move forward with this solution.

Learning goal 1: Identify which support channels users find most valuable, from our list of feasible solutions.

Methodology: This will be an asynchronous ranking task for about 50 users. We will present users with our five solution candidate options and ask them to rank them in order of preference. We will also include an indicator for "would not use" as an option and an opportunity for additional comments.

Recruitment: We will be offering a small incentive ($10 account credit) and sending a participation link to a sample group of users who have opted in for research participation.

Share-out: Solutions will be presented in order of overall preference score and score distribution. Insightful comments will also be highlighted in a summary document.

Obviously, this is not the only methodology a team might use to learn this information. The important thing for the team is that they have a clear learning goal and a shared agreement about what kind of evidence is worthwhile in making the next decisions.

Stories Tied to Features

Once a solution has been chosen and a feature is created (tied to an epic, of course), any further research or design stories can now be attached to that feature, such as any solution validation stories that a team uses to test a feature with users prior to launch.

Estimating, Planning, and Scheduling Specific HCD Activities

Interviews take time. Wireframes take time. Research and design are no different than other work the team does—the work itself needs to be agreed on, estimated, and delivered, just like any development work. It is also important for dependencies to be accounted for.

So, how long does it take? "It depends." That is the first answer given by any HCD practitioner when asked how long work will take. Designers are famous for it. Good estimation requires a discussion that happens with Designers based on their particular skills and the problems they are being asked to solve, as well as the tools and resources they have available at the outset. (It turns out Designers are a lot like developers that way).

Generally, however, in order to fully deliver the value of Human-Centered Agile, backlogs need to be stable enough to reflect approximately 3–6 sprints (typically 6–12 weeks) worth of upcoming standard work, with more lead time to account for high-complexity and/or high-stakes work that may take longer to research and design.

Discovery Work (Estimate: 1–4 Sprints)

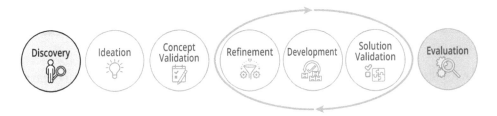

Discovery work means talking to users to learn what they want. If users are nearby and the necessary learning is narrow, this might only require a few days to conduct interviews and synthesize findings. However, some discovery work can take multiple sprints (weeks or months) to plan and conduct if teams

- have a harder-to-reach audience without enough established, understood information (this is especially true if travel is required).
- have open-ended (exploratory) learning goals or more narrowly focused goals of specific problem validation.

Depending on the learning goals, the team will estimate how long it would take to prepare, conduct, and analyze the types of interviews or other work that will procure the necessary answers.

Ideation (Estimate: 1 Sprint)

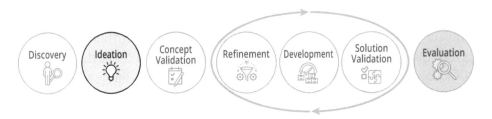

Ideation involves taking what is known about users and business stakeholders and determining how to solve their problem or serve their needs (sometimes referred to as "How might we?"). This means deciding what type of solution is best for the job and understanding what that solution might look like in reality. To do this, the team must determine the acceptable range of solutions—and because there is already a clear idea of what users will want and how to determine success from prior steps, selecting the solution becomes a matter of figuring out which will most effectively deliver results within the amount of time and energy the business is willing to invest. It's important to remember that this ideation effort is still a fairly "big picture" effort.

The example ideation story earlier in the chapter, for producing additional support channels, might produce several candidate solutions:

■ An FAQ page and a help@yourcompany.com email address
■ A form with questions that have pre-defined answers or open text fields with auto-population
■ A live chat session with a support professional
■ Artificial intelligence/bot-based support that can learn to respond effectively to customers using a wide range of digital data sources to provide answers
■ A stand-alone support app that includes self-service information and location-based issue reporting capabilities, including photo/video uploads

Obviously, the listed solution examples are not comprehensive, nor do they consider proactive support measures, such as scheduled outreach to customers. It is clear that the range of effort in designing and delivering each can vary wildly.

For the simplest solutions, teams could expect most of the ideation to be completed within a single sprint (maybe a couple of days). This is a common outcome but not a certain one. As solution ideas get more complex (and have fewer well-defined conventions to borrow), the conceptual design of specific features can take longer—in this example, the support app would take longer to design.

AN AGILE FRAMEWORK FOR DECOMPOSING AND ESTIMATING DESIGN CONCEPTS

No matter how design is done, a design concept will always need to move from "big picture" to a more refined state during refinement into stories and acceptance criteria so developers can deliver it. Moving from a low-fidelity concept design that will require multiple states and outcomes can be challenging, and teams may not have the same level of confidence estimating low-fidelity/low-maturity design work as they do when estimating other work. In fact, teams routinely look to Designers for a perfect, on-the-spot estimate at the concept stage or simply assign a deadline (which is the least Agile approach possible).

Once teams have a design concept for a feature, it's time to conduct the *design* sizing activity. This is either done collaboratively by the entire delivery team, or by a subset of the team that must include the Product Owner, Designers, and members who can speak to any identified technical and business constraints.

- Step 1: Document assumptions and evaluate stakes.
- Step 2: Create a shared reference point.
- Step 3: Decompose design into smaller units of work.
- Step 4: Discuss design risks for each unit of work.
- Step 5: Conduct planning poker for sizing.

STEP 1: DOCUMENT ASSUMPTIONS AND EVALUATE STAKES

Teams that have completed a vision workshop should already have a sense of how well they actually know their users. Teams need to consider their assumptions about their users, how they derived their knowledge of their users, whether there are gaps in that knowledge (particularly as it pertains to the problems they are proposing to solve), how familiar they are with the types of products and solutions users might accept, and, most important, how they will handle any mistakes or misjudgments.

With those things in mind, teams can ask any clarifying questions of their stakeholders, plan the kind of research work required to address any areas of uncertainty and risky assumptions about the user before moving on.

STEP 2: CREATE A SHARED VISUAL REFERENCE

It is crucial to have a shared visual reference describing the conceptual design. This can be as low fidelity as whiteboard drawings or a more detailed wireframe or mock-up. The key is for everyone to have the same basic picture in their head of what is getting delivered. This is critical for setting agreements on feasibility and managing expectations around what, how, and when will be delivered.

STEP 3: DECOMPOSE DESIGN INTO SMALLER UNITS OF WORK

Just as with other story decomposition, teams should seek other ways to decompose work to make it easier to assess, such as the ability to meaningfully separate any screens or interactions and the dependency of related features.

STEP 4: DISCUSS DESIGN RISKS FOR EACH UNIT OF WORK

For each story, teams must discuss the design risks. They should consider things, such as if there are interactions that are hard to find, if users will be able to identify primary and secondary actions, and whether there is some form of redress if they make mistakes. Having this discussion of design risks becomes a starting point for building the eventual acceptance criteria for stories that get delivered.

STEP 5: MEETING PARTICIPANTS ESTIMATE DESIGNS FOR THE SIZE OF DESIGN EFFORT

Whether using planning poker for design estimation or something simpler like T-shirt sizes, it is important to be able to set a rough expectation of how long each piece of design work will take for planning purposes. This allows the team to plan the correct amount of time for design work ahead of the refinement sessions for stories that require those designs. For a comprehensive discussion of estimation techniques, see Mike Cohn's *Agile Estimating and Planning*, referenced in the recommended reading section.

Concept Validation (Estimate: 1–2 Sprints)

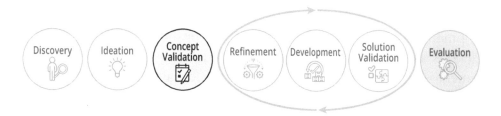

Human-Centered Agile means planning to learn from users to mitigate the risk of building unwanted products. Teams should plan for concept validation based on the stakes of building a proposed feature, in time and either cost of delivery or cost in terms of reputation or lost opportunity if a rollout goes poorly.

In the previous example, the team would likely not need to conduct a concept validation on the phone or email solutions and might consider it for a form-based solution (particularly for those that require building a high number of forms, forms with a great deal of logic, or a large amount of time or sensitive information from the user in order to complete). It would be a mistake to build a chat solution if the customer only feels comfortable speaking directly to a representative, especially when providing sensitive information, or a specialized app if the customer cannot imagine needing or using a standalone, single-purpose app for rare support occasions.

As with all testing, the amount of effort will be determined by what needs to be learned. The methodology should be driven by the specific learning need, and the effort level should be driven by the stakes of the outcomes (is a prototype required, or can the learning be accomplished simply through interviews or even a focus group session?).

Refinement (Estimate: 1–2 Sprints)

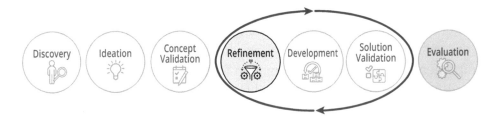

Refinement is where HCD and conventional Agile development collaborate most directly. As stories get refined to the point that they can be worked on by developers, specific design artifacts may be created to support the development effort, such as wireframes or screenshots that depict specific interactions, behaviors, and outcomes. This can typically occur while the refinement itself is happening (1–2 sprints ahead), although more complex designs and interactions may take longer.

Solution Validation (Estimate: 1–3 Sprints)

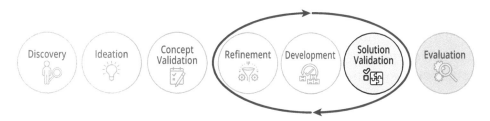

Ordinarily, solution validation occurs in the form of usability testing. As with earlier research, the required time varies based on how organized user recruiting is done, how much learning must take place from usability testing, and how rigorous that testing needs to be in order to achieve the desired learning outcomes.

For example, a team may wish to do the equivalent of a usability "smoke test" that shows users a new feature to ensure they understand its purpose and can do basic task completion. This is different from "functional testing" in that the user is provided a task but not the scripted set of actions to complete it. This highlights navigational concerns or gaps, especially when every function is working properly, but users get stuck on determining the correct path forward. This kind of task might inform a "go/no-go" decision and be relatively fast to conduct. The learning objective is simply to be reassured that users will not flood the product support team with confused questions.

Alternatively, a team may wish to learn more comprehensively about how users experience a complex process, the resulting emotion (frustration or delight), or specific steps, interactions, pieces of language, or supporting features that would improve an experience. Diving deeper into additional questions and more involved behavior paths takes longer in setup, implementation, and analysis.

Evaluation (Estimate: 1–2 Sprints)

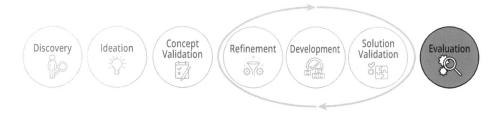

Evaluation is an essential aspect of Human-Centered Agile because, without measuring releases, it will be nearly impossible to determine whether the solution being created achieves the intended outcomes. Human-Centered Agile means evaluating products and bringing insights back into the overall product strategy so that teams can make good choices about how to invest their efforts in generating the desired outcomes.

Evaluation takes the same kind of planning and preparation as other research work. Whatever teams do to measure success (hopefully defined earlier in the process) will take work, which needs to be planned as well. The key difference here is that some planning for evaluation work can be done during the time that development is taking place, but because evaluation will not take place until after a release, some planning will have to wait. For example, recruiting should only take place after release is certain, and test scripts must reflect the final released product.

Using Estimates to Plan HCD Work

As with any Agile work, that estimation and planning come from the team and are revalidated and tracked as the team measures the team output and outcomes of the work itself. Any discovery, ideation, and concept or solution validation efforts must take place in advance of a release, sometimes several sprints ahead, so the results can be successfully incorporated by the development team. The order of the steps matters. Teams in usability testing don't want to discover that they are solving the wrong problem or have the wrong kind of solution altogether, especially after putting in substantial work to deliver a product. They may learn exactly that if they have not done discovery or ideation work and are only doing validation via usability testing just prior to release, for example.

Consider Additional Dependent Workflows

Not all types of work that take place ahead of implementation have the same stakeholders or effort level. Visual design may or may not require coordination with other stakeholders, such as creative teams or brand managers that provide feedback or approval. The life cycle and workflow of content creation can be notoriously difficult, with a variety of stakeholders weighing in (legal departments, marketing teams, etc.). Dependencies that have a separate workflow and approval process are notorious for tripping up teams that wait until they are nearing release to make sure that these needs are met.

Additionally, marketing or communications often requires parallel work so products are launched with proper marketing and customer support. When planning release work, each may warrant a separate roadmap and backlog for tracking work in progress.

HCD within Agile Events

In addition to planning and executing HCD-specific stories, it is helpful to think about what an HCD practitioner's role is during typical Agile events. While HCD practitioners are equal participants no different than any other, they are specifically tasked with representing the users' interests more directly than other roles are. Because of this, they are likely to have different sorts of questions and input than other team members.

HCD at Sprint Planning: Asking Questions to Adjust Focus

Too often at sprint or iteration planning, the "ready, fire, aim" pattern is executed, even by mature teams. Having an HCD practitioner participate in both sprint planning and its companion event, backlog refinement, is helpful because they ask thought-provoking questions, like

- Has the team probed the user to find out why they want this and discover if there are latent needs?
- What would happen if the team solved the users' problem in a different way? Has the team considered multiple solution approaches and evaluated them for cost, flexibility, and desirability?
- How can the team set up an inexpensive Minimum Viable Product that can be built quickly, then validate with actual end users that this solution is acceptable before further investment is made?
- Is the team sure their proposed solution follows the patterns that already exist in the product and won't confuse users?
- Has the team created a visualization of the solution to ensure that Product Owners and the delivery team truly have the same outcome in mind?
- Has the team identified that the solution uses best design practices (e.g., error handling, interaction feedback, clear visual hierarchy, etc.)?

■ Has the team created an evaluation plan that maps back to user sentiment or user behaviors? (Too often, feature delivery is the yardstick for
success, without regard for outcomes.)

HCD at Story Generation and Story Refinement

The typical role for HCD at story refinement is like their role in sprint planning but with a longer timeframe and more strategic view. HCD practitioners
can add value during story refinement precisely because the items being
considered during this meeting won't be in scope for at least another sprint.
HCD practitioners have time to gather and apply insight to these items and
get them "ready" before the next sprint planning session.

GROUP DESIGN CRITIQUE IN HUMAN-CENTERED AGILE

There are two points in the process where the team is most likely to
come together to review and critique designs: following ideation, when
there are low-fidelity design concepts, and during refinement, when granular decisions about what a solution will look like and how it will behave
get decided. In either case, the team should consider making "design
critique" part of the story agreement. For ideation stories, this can mean
saying that critique and final agreement are necessary as part of the
definition of done. For stories that are in refinement for development,
especially those that reflect the implementation of new designs, critique
might be included as part of the definition of ready.

WHEN TO CRITIQUE DESIGN AS A GROUP

One of the genuine challenges of bringing any kind of design (HCD or
otherwise) is to get non-Designer stakeholders to consider design from
a broader perspective instead of aesthetic appreciation. "Can we make it
cleaner? Can we make it *pop*?"

These statements represent a personal aesthetic preference and
shouldn't be the basis of an actionable design critique. Getting stuck in
a preference-based feedback cycle puts Designers in the difficult spot of
prioritizing one person's aesthetic preferences over any other key considerations of a design. To solve this, teams can implement a clear, four-step

design review and critique process that fundamentally addresses whether a design is likely to produce its intended outcomes.

STEP 1: "DESIGN PROBLEM" ORIENTATION

Start with an orientation before showing any design. The moment people see a picture, they only think about the picture. Instead, discuss the problems the design is meant to solve and outcomes it is meant to drive. Describe the behaviors the design is meant to encourage in the customer. Write the problem and intended outcomes down somewhere that remains in view as the design itself is being discussed. It may also be valuable to post other orienting pieces of information (such as personas or journey maps) if they are important to understanding specific design decisions.

STEP 2: "DESIGN PROCESS" ORIENTATION

This step should also precede showing designs. Be explicit about the following aspects of the design: fidelity, maturity, and proximity (see Chapter 3). Talk about what kind of shared agreement to build and whether that is around the right problem, the right solution, or done right. If stakeholders aren't yet familiar with the difference between fidelity and maturity, set clear expectations. It is easy for design critiques to go off the rails when stakeholders get caught up on the wrong level of problem or design detail.

STEP 3: DESIGN PRESENTATION

Present the design without taking questions. Ask stakeholders to write down their notes for later discussion. Walk through the complete design sequentially and discuss the decision-making and methodology behind it. What choices were made and why? How do they support the outcome described in Step 1? Can the Designer describe their choices in the language of design (e.g., pointing out decisions that support better wayfinding, affordance, or any other aspect of experience essential for success)?

STEP 4: DISCUSSION

Just as it sounds, this is the opportunity for each person with questions or comments to have them addressed. Ask that questions be framed in terms of how effective it is at solving the stated problem. Aesthetics matter, but be clear about how the aesthetic approach does or doesn't contribute to what is meant to be accomplished. Like any other facilitated exercise, it is important to manage the conversation so that as many questions get addressed as possible and specific concerns are heard.

Additionally, as the discussion progresses (and alternatives inevitably get proposed), be willing to ask, "What are the stakes of this particular decision? How much impact would an alternative decision have here?" This will help avoid long discussions about simple preferences for smaller design details.

ADDITIONAL CONSIDERATIONS FOR CRITIQUE

There are a few aspects that are easily missed or forgotten in any design evaluation. The great tendency is to review a design for how effective it is at solving its specific problem, which is the first and most important consideration of a design, but it is also important to understand the context that it will fit within.

It is worth asking questions about how context-appropriate the design is and how flexible it will be in responding to future updates.

- How will the design scale if needed? If content or specific elements change, will the overall design flex to accommodate them?
- When working within a design standard, is the design in line with those standards?
- Is this design reusable, and are there candidates for new design patterns?

Wrap up by making it clear which feedback can be taken by the Designer as *suggestions* for improvement and which are considered *requirements* for release.

RUNNING A CRITIQUE SESSION COVERING MULTIPLE DESIGNS

Running a critique that is meant to cover more than one design can be risky but often necessary for scheduling and availability reasons. The challenge is to make sure that the entire session is not subsumed by a single discussion. To accomplish that, we recommend a couple of strategies:

- Have a visible agenda for the designs being critiqued during the session. As each is addressed, mark that critique complete.
- Timebox each critique, and, when a specific discussion hits its limit, have the team vote to move on or continue based on urgency.

Sprint Review: Receiving Incremental Feedback

While some teams use this opportunity to provide meaningful feedback, the sprint review is often something of a ceremonial effort—work that has already been agreed to and seen by the Product Owner is being triumphantly rolled out to a wider stakeholder set. Progress and burn-down charts are reviewed. Sometimes there's no mention of what's next on the roadmap. *This isn't how it is supposed to be.*

The sprint review is a fantastic opportunity to hear from critical stakeholders about the experience. If they are encouraged to ask questions or report experiences, HCD practitioners might help elicit further insights to incorporate into future iterations, become part of the persona/scenario documentation, or simply strengthen relationships that facilitate access to users. An "open conversation"–style sprint review is also likely to build stakeholder confidence in the product being built, as design decisions and trade-offs can be negotiated.

Sprint Retrospective: Supporting Process Improvement

The sprint retrospective is another area of the Agile process that meshes well with HCD thinking and methods. The retrospective is common to all Agile frameworks and a key part of why Agile is so successful. If the team can incorporate learning, remove impediments, and otherwise optimize their process every two weeks, they will improve over time, like interest compounds in a savings account. The shorter the sprint, the more rapidly the "interest" compounds.

Typically, teams have no difficulty recognizing the biggest or most important process-related problems to solve. Once identified, teams analyze them to find their root causes and then brainstorm possible solutions. Their goal is to come up with a story that will improve their biggest problem or remove their biggest impediment.

The inventory of the things teams do to identify problems and root causes and brainstorm possible solutions is remarkably similar to what HCD practitioners do regularly. HCD practitioners are well suited to adding value to the process by encouraging conversation and capturing team responses.

LARGER PROGRAMS, DIFFERENT NEEDS

Chapter 8

Managing Distributed Design Efforts in Agile

As teams and programs grow into multiple teams and then into scaled operations, new needs and complexities enter the picture. The first natural phase of growth within a program is to go from a single team to a few small teams that work together. If the work is broken up so these teams are *truly* independent, scaling HCD looks like planning and incorporating HCD activities using a Research Roadmap, with a review of HCD work to evaluate stakes. That is to say, when teams are working on products that aren't dependent on one another or the dependencies are limited enough to handle informally, they can continue working independently; they will *each* own a product roadmap, a Research Roadmap that captures the supporting HCD efforts, and their own design and research standards specific to their work.

As teams start to work in common product ecosystems or solutions, they must update their approach. This becomes especially apparent if they experience problems with the design consistency of products and solutions that are delivered by different teams. In digital products, this usually takes several forms; inconsistent fonts, graphics, or copy style from one screen to another; varying interaction design, which leads to multiple ways of completing basic tasks (such as entering addresses uniformly), or confusing delivery of feedback and error messages. This can even result in situations where users are unsure whether they are within a single experience ("Wait, is this a different site?"). Less drastic inconsistencies can lead users to question product credibility or can require extra learning time with new features.

DOI: 10.4324/9781003188520-12

HCD Practitioners working on different teams need a way for their work to be consistent. If products are related, design choices should reflect that and the only way to achieve that is through the active orchestration of these teams. In practice, this can range from the guidance that teams may deviate from based on their own judgment to much more rigid governance that requires centralized design approval.

When starting to handle distributed design work, product teams usually attempt to establish basic design standards first, if they aren't already in place. At the previous single-team level, design standards, based on the degree of specificity required, were often captured into style guides or pattern libraries to maintain consistency. The purpose of these documents at the previous level was primarily *longitudinal*, the team wanted to make sure its future decisions were consistent with past decisions. Additionally, they may have developed artifacts for efficiency, such as reusable templates to articulate designs more quickly.

When the organization moves to distributed work, the concern over maintaining consistency is no longer primarily longitudinal, it is also *latitudinal*. A decision made by one team, affecting the overall design ecosystem, needs to be agreed to and assimilated by other design teams as efficiently as possible. Otherwise, competing design approaches start to emerge.

Consistency of Product Design

The goal of design ops is to give Designers at the team level enough independence and flexibility to solve the specific problems in front of them while ensuring that their designs are appropriate for the context in which they will be deployed.

Design consistency refers to consistency in *all* facets of the design:

- **Visual**—using the same colors, fonts, and font sizes
- **Interaction**—uniform product appearance, behavior, and error management from one user to another
- **Content and Voice**—standardized vocabulary and voice across the product portfolio

Depending on the environment, teams may have multiple stakeholders for product design. Someone should track the use of brand elements, such as colors, logos, and so on, as well as whether there are policy or legal constraints on how the material is used. Making sure new designs reflect a good product vision and adhere to any other constraints is critical to getting products out the door.

Tools for Ensuring Consistency across Teams

It's very possible that current documentation is simply definitional, such as the use of certain color values or font-specific indicators. As a single team, ongoing discussions about how and when to use these elements—what makes for good uses of accent colors, or different heading styles—is important but likely happened naturally within the flow of product design and implementation. As a distributed team, being able to refer to decisions that multiple teams contribute to and have a stake in is essential.

If a team is already using a style guide or pattern library, moving to a distributed team requires evolving this documentation. In addition to the style *definition* (e.g., what different headers look like in terms of font family and size), documentation should now include style *guidance* as well (such as when it is appropriate to use each header). Guidance is reviewed with new Designers to ensure they understand how patterns are meant to be applied.

If the teams have not yet started using style guides and pattern libraries, it is now essential that they develop them. For larger programs that would benefit from a more robust centralized design, two new concepts, code libraries and design systems, deliver higher levels of detail and efficiency, as the front-end code gets incorporated into the centrally maintained design resources.

Code Libraries—A set of code developed to render designs consistently in a repeatable way and promote code reuse. They are often, but not always, built on a specific front-end framework—a common code base usually mixing HTML, CSS, and JavaScript that creates consistent appearance and behaviors (examples include Bootstrap, developed by Twitter, or Material-UI, based on Google's Material Design).

Design Systems—A tool meant to fully aggregate styles, patterns, code, and guidance (including high-level design principles) into a managed and implementable system. By creating a design system, teams give their Designers tools that should help them allocate more time to the harder parts of the design process. At the level of distributed teams, teams may find it useful to create an early and very basic design system. To see a couple of example design systems, check out IBM's Carbon Design System[1] or Shopify's Polaris Design System.[2]

Design Governance

As with any standard practice, there are pros and cons to creating design standards that Designers are expected to follow. On one hand, products will look and behave in a consistent fashion, more closely reflecting an organizational sensibility about what the product(s) should be. Design standards also provide guidance on micro-level design decisions, such as how to handle specific repeating interactions and apply specified visual styles. This enables teams to produce higher-fidelity designs more quickly.

On the other hand, design systems themselves require a maintenance investment, and individual teams or Designers may feel overly limited in what they are able to produce. Depending on the team culture and constraints of stakeholder obligations, teams must determine the correct level of governance to complement their standards.

There is no one "right" level of detail for a style guide or pattern library. The "right" level of detail is that which works across all the teams. However, the three most common ways to handle this are:

Voluntary Compliance—This approach, often appropriate for small teams, produces standards but allows compliance to be fully voluntary at the team level. In other words, Designers have a tool set to choose from (or not) as they wish, and the determination about what is "good enough" consistency happens at a team level. This avoids the headache of any additional overhead that goes into governance. However, unenforced standards will likely lead to more consistency but not perfect consistency.

Centralized Design Reviews and Approval—Creating a centralized review and approval process is the next step toward creating more consistency. Designs are reviewed for standards compliance *before* they are implemented by the developers. Designers will typically present proposed designs for evaluation that, as part of that evaluation process, will be vetted for whether they do or do not adhere to established standards.

External Design Reviews and Approval—If an organization requires additional stakeholders to review any portion of the design or copy, teams will also want those approvals to happen before a design is considered "ready."

---

[1] https://carbondesignsystem.com/
[2] https://polaris.shopify.com/design

Coordinated Design Activities

Collaborative Ideation

If the program is growing from a single team to distributed teams, the process of collaborative ideation may need to change. What may have previously been ideation conducted through ad hoc conversations, story refinement, and other informal means, now needs to incorporate additional interests, specifically

- additional stakeholders from other Agile teams because of cross-team dependencies or impacts (or even needs).
- user research conducted on behalf of other teams to help in ideation.

In order to ensure that the stakeholders are involved and that user understanding is maximized, collaborative ideation should become a more formal process. One particularly effective way to accomplish this is to do collaborative ideation as a workshop.

Reviewing and Accepting Stories

As stories are elaborated and questions answered, teams need a way to know when a story has enough definition for them to begin working on it. Many teams adopt a "definition of ready" or a "ready checklist" to help keep them from pulling stories into a sprint that they don't know enough about to complete. In order to maintain consistency across teams, the definition of ready should include "designs have been reviewed for compliance with design standards" before they are deemed acceptable for development.

PRO TIP: CREATE A READY CHECKLIST

Many successful Agile teams have adopted the pattern of the "ready checklist" in order to know if a story contains enough information and is ready to be brought into sprint planning. This checklist also ensures that the team has had enough time to consider their approach. Teams should talk about a story no less than three times at backlog refinement before considering it "ready."

Story refinement is the perfect time to consider spike stories for any research needed to support the work. Because these stories have not been started, HCD practitioners have time to build the Research Roadmap needed to support them.

A ready checklist might look something like what is shown in Figure 8.1.

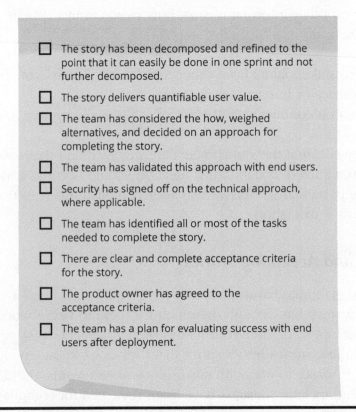

☐ The story has been decomposed and refined to the point that it can easily be done in one sprint and not further decomposed.

☐ The story delivers quantifiable user value.

☐ The team has considered the how, weighed alternatives, and decided on an approach for completing the story.

☐ The team has validated this approach with end users.

☐ Security has signed off on the technical approach, where applicable.

☐ The team has identified all or most of the tasks needed to complete the story.

☐ There are clear and complete acceptance criteria for the story.

☐ The product owner has agreed to the acceptance criteria.

☐ The team has a plan for evaluating success with end users after deployment.

Figure 8.1   An example ready checklist.

Just because a story is ready doesn't mean it is a priority or that it will ever be done at all. It simply means that the team has enough information to pull it into a sprint should it be prioritized.

It is important to have some stories ready and know which stories actually are ready, because as the team gets better at retrospectives and continuously improves their process, they will start finishing early. When teams start finishing early, it is important to have a backlog of ready stories, as the teams won't have to pause and can keep value flowing by taking the highest priority item and working on it earlier than planned.

The Designer Sync Meeting

Whether teams treat this as an official ceremony or unofficial activity, Designers should meet periodically (once or twice a sprint is typical) to review each other's in-progress designs. This meeting should cover designs that are both in the ideation process and in the refinement process. The goal of this meeting is similar to design critique but differs in that it is an *internal* meeting of Designers reviewing work as peers.

During this meeting, Designers review each other's work to ensure

■ that high-quality designs are being produced that address the problems their teams are trying to solve.

■ that designs are consistent, comply with design standards, and fit within the overall design ecosystem.

Maintaining and Updating Standards

Team standards documents are living documents. Don't expect that it is possible for every Designer to know every style or pattern up front. As individual teams work on new design challenges, they run into situations in which existing design patterns don't provide quite enough support and that team will want to create new patterns that can impact design standards used by all teams. At other times, patterns will need updating or splitting into peer patterns. Every so often, even with the most robust of standards-compliant governance processes, a team decides that there is an excellent reason not to use an established standard and leave a one-off exception in its place.

It is impossible to deal with all these additional needs in the heat of the day-to-day story-level design activities that go along with supporting teams. Specific activities are needed to ensure they happen. Therefore, teams must reserve some portion of their capacity for such activities.

Design Operations

It is worth noting that management of design standards falls under the general umbrella of design operations ("design ops"), which is a rich topic outside the scope of this book. However, to ensure comprehension of the content that is within the scope of this book, a high-level overview follows.

The Nielsen Norman Group[3] describes design ops as "the orchestration and optimization of people, processes, and craft in order to amplify design's value and impact at scale."[4]

Design ops encompasses all the support and scaffolding activities surrounding the basic delivery of design but not as part of the design itself. For the purposes here, this means:

- Any activity that goes into the creation, maintenance, and documentation of standards, whether they are simple style guides, fully articulated design systems that require updates to code, or anything in between
- Any activity performed for the specific reason of ensuring standards compliance. This includes cross-team design reviews to help evaluate standards compliance or identify candidate updates (such as new patterns or system components). It also includes any review sessions with external stakeholders to ensure products are appropriate for release.
- Any effort spent managing the tools of design. In order to make sure designs can be worked on collaboratively across teams, it is important that teams use the same tool stack, including whatever tools are being used to generate design, share out design, and manage version control.
- Any effort spent creating and managing the processes that Designers use, such as design charters and cross-team creative reviews or design critiques
- Any effort spent on recruiting, onboarding, and offboarding Designers

When creating a design organization, these subjects are important. This book is interested in integrating program-level activities at the right point but will not be covering the full scope of design ops. For an excellent introduction to the topic, see *Org Design for Design Orgs* by Peter Merholz and Kristin Skinner.[5]

---

[3] www.nngroup.com—The Nielsen Norman Group was founded by Jakob Nielsen and Donald Norman and is a wealth of articles and resources about user experience.
[4] www.nngroup.com/articles/design-operations-101/
[5] Peter Merholz and Kristin Skinner, 2016, *Org Design for Design Orgs*, O'Reilly Media, Inc

Chapter 9

Managing Distributed Research Efforts in Agile

Just as Designers working on different teams need a way for their work to be consistent with one another, researchers also need coordination to avoid redundant work and ensure their work brings maximum value.

While design is about ensuring consistency, research coordination is about providing a better view of upcoming efforts for planning and prioritization, creating standards and templates to make individual research activities more consistent and efficient, centralizing specific support activities such as recruiting, and sharing value from captured insights for use across teams and efforts.

Outgrowing Ad Hoc Research

When working as a single and fully independent Agile team, it is straightforward to plan and conduct research needed for their own operations. Any insights live within that one team, either in formal capture documents (personas and journey maps) or in an informal collective shared understanding.

In a sense, a single team's research efforts can be thought of as a *bespoke* approach. The research is designed to meet the team's individual needs and serve them in their decision-making on a case-by-case basis. Findings may also become part of their foundational shared understanding of their users or vision, as the team plans, conducts, synthesizes, and shares their work.

DOI: 10.4324/9781003188520-13

By contrast, in a distributed environment, research is conducted by one team that may be valuable to other teams with interest in similar users or use cases.

Teams may be able to maintain this research approach after work is distributed across teams, if

- the amount of research happening is already "right sized" to the team (i.e., there aren't idle researchers or more work than those researchers can handle).
- the teams' research domains are independent enough that their exploratory research and solution validation insights would not be valuable to each other.
- the teams' participant pools are independent of one another, and teams can be sure not to accidentally overtax participants.

Conversely, teams will find a need to coordinate research activities when gaining insights that should be shared across efforts, experiencing resource challenges in prioritizing or conducting research, or sharing a common participant pool.

At the point where research needs to be coordinated across multiple teams, several efforts must be initiated, including:

- Coordinated research efforts, including recruiting and shared tools and templates
- A learning strategy
- A Research Roadmap
- An insights repository

Coordinated Research Efforts

Just as design ops encompasses all the support and scaffolding activities surrounding the basic delivery of design, research operations (research ops) involve the tools and processes needed by researchers to conduct their research. As the number of practitioners and teams grows, teams require processes that support multiple people doing coordinated work.

Coordinated Recruitment and Messaging

As participant recruitment is managed, it is important that teams are consistent in the language they use to interact with users and their frequency of contact. This maintains the credibility of the organization and preserves user willingness to participate.

Recruiting a Common Participant Pool

If teams need the same participants, it does not make sense to have fully independent recruitment efforts. A larger pool of participants from which users are drawn is better than two separate, smaller pools. Additionally, a common pool lessens the burden (per team) of generating their own participants while avoiding the potential for the same candidate participant to be contacted with an initial outreach campaign more than once.

Participation Rate per Participant

Despite the level of enthusiasm, participating in research can be an anxiety-producing, tiring experience. Given a small pool of participation candidates for any reason (e.g., the product has a specialized set of users or teams still have a fairly small reach), teams will want to make sure they don't overtax their ability to meaningfully contribute. Teams that reach out to the same people too often can suffer precipitous drops in participation rates (not unlike "survey fatigue").

Common Voice

Like any other communications channel, communications with research participants should feel as if they come from one single organization, not different individuals. This means

- sending out invitations that sound similar to one another.
- having a common communication cadence—frequency and timing of reminders, follow-up communications, and so on.
- ensuring any rules and standards are well explained, no matter the team or the effort.

Common Standards and Expectations

It is critical to clearly define practices and procedures, such as participation incentives, the management of collected data, and participant privacy. Participants should have a clear understanding of what their commitment is. These considerations must be accounted for in addition to the experience feeling familiar to repeat participants. This is why it is important to confirm that standards and guidelines are in place and followed.

Tools and Templates

There are many research processes and artifacts to coordinate to remain consistent from effort to effort. This is particularly true of recruiting artifacts, such as:

- Policies
- Engagement process
- Communications templates
- Research plans
- Scripts
- Tools for conducting research
- Synthesis
- Share outs

Policies

Policies include decisions about whether sessions are recorded and what happens to those recordings, how customer privacy is handled, what the incentive policy is for participation, and whether and when any sort of non-disclosure agreement (NDA) or business protection is required.

Engagement Process

Whether research requests come from leadership (such as with "exploration and innovation" efforts) or from teams to validate or evaluate solutions, key stakeholders need to know what to expect from the research process in terms of the time and effort required to conduct and synthesize research in order to plan accordingly. Without a clear and shared understanding of the research process, teams will be saddled with unrealistic turnarounds or research requests that don't align to the actual learning goals.

Communications Templates

Teams should also have standard templates for communicating with participants. Templates ensure that necessary information is clearly and consistently conveyed. Templates also ensure that there is a singular organizational voice, which is important for trust and credibility. In addition to participant-facing communications, teams may need to create scripts and templates for use in dealing with stakeholders to make sure that they are consistently addressing the information needs of those stakeholders by including details that are relevant to them specifically.

Research Plans

A research plan identifies the purpose and scope of research and keeps individual research efforts on track. It should identify the learning goals of the research, as well as the methodology, milestones, and timeframe. It should also include the share-out audiences and deliverables to present findings.

Scripts

When conducting specific tests, teams should keep the participant experience consistent—the idea is for each participant to have the same understanding of what is happening and respond to the same questions and prompts. This is particularly true as the rigor of study increases—exploratory interviews that happen in discovery may start with the same basic initial prompts but leave plenty of room for the interviewer to decide how to follow up, whereas in validation/evaluation efforts, users should be given identical tasks. There is also orienting information that every participant should know at the outset, such as how long their involvement will take, what it entails, and how to end a session if they need to for any reason. A script ensures all of this is appropriately communicated.

Tools for Conducting Research and Synthesizing Findings

While research methodologies can vary wildly in complexity—ranging from sessions with users that involve no more than interview scripts and paper prototypes to watching people interact with fully developed products—teams working separately will benefit from using the same tools as one another. All teams engaged in asynchronous remote testing, for example, should use the same tool. Similarly, whatever the process is for synthesizing research, the platform or tools used should be common across the organization.

Share-Outs

There should be an established process for researchers to share any insights gathered with their teams. It is important to develop and use templates for the artifacts that capture these insights, as well as to ensure there are presentations and meetings involving the proper stakeholders in the effort.

THE "BITE, SNACK, MEAL" APPROACH TO SHARE-OUTS

As with many design efforts, there is no objectively correct way to capture and document research findings for the stakeholders that will consume them immediately. Deliverables can be as detailed as a multiple-page research report that reads like an academic paper, describing the methodology with precision and results in great detail, or as high level as a slide deck with a few bullet points.

Our general recommendation, when summarizing artifacts, is to go with what we call the "bite, snack, meal" approach, where each level has a different goal.

The "bite" is the equivalent of an executive summary. Its purpose is to briefly demonstrate the key or highest-impact conclusions reached (the ones a team is most likely to act on that make major changes to the product or strategy). This does not need to include every insight or even most of them. This document is a page or less, the methodology is described only briefly, and conclusions are bolstered with quotes and top-level statistics. The goal of this document is to inform strategy conversations with research study findings, without getting into every finding or method used.

The "snack" provides the more directly invested stakeholders with a fuller sense of what the research determined. This deliverable tends to be a 2–3-page report summary that dives deeper into the research goals and methodology used. While still not comprehensive, it offers a more expansive summary of the insights gathered, such as high-value data tables or other in-depth synthesis outcomes.

The "meal" is the full research report, which includes a detailed breakdown of methodology (and specific artifacts used), the complete set of synthesized findings, and the associated raw data (if requested). This exists so that any stakeholder can dive as deeply as desired to investigate the conclusions and feel comfortable with (or possibly critique) the methodology. This document provides the transparency a team requires for credibility and collaboration.

As with design artifacts, this documentation is not intended to create unnecessary overhead for a team. Rather, the underlying goal is to meet stakeholders at their level of abstraction, so they can receive the full value of the team's work and findings. Any documents not serving that purpose should be cut from the overall efforts.

An Insight Repository

The goal of an insight repository is to capture findings in a way that makes them accessible and easy to consume across teams and time. An insight repository is a bit different from a share-out since it is meant to be explorable and informative to the teams doing related work, not drive specific, time-bound decisions.

An "Insight" is the Atomic Unit of the Insight Repository

An insight is a research-supported claim about the attitudes, behaviors, or expectations that (all or specific) users have. For a repository, HCD practitioners want to extract any insights demonstrated in research and bring them forward as claims that have been tested in some way. This is not to say that a research repository will not include the foundational data or full reports, just that the teams are primarily looking for the insights themselves (and not long detailed reports that require examination), which is why it is organized this way.

The insight repository needs to be built to accomplish three things:

1. **Stakeholders can see key information at the first view.** In addition to the insight itself, this should include details about the research, like the date, method, and relevant context, as well as the product for which the insight was generated, and the question that the research sought to answer. This is not an exhaustive list. Some teams may find that they are doing research tailored to specific personas or specific

moments within a journey. Any facets relevant to the organization for searching insights would go here.

2. **Stakeholders can locate the generated reports related to the insight.** Whether these are contained in the insight repository or elsewhere, this information should be available for stakeholders wanting a more complete picture of how the research was conducted and the conclusions reached.

3. **Connect the insight repository to the learning strategy.** The insight repository connects to the learning strategy in two key ways. The first should be obvious—if teams are missing basic information for their strategy, they may find that a well-organized repository can provide the necessary clarification. The second is that a learning strategy should inform the content organization of the repository, so there is a holistic approach to deciding what needs to be learned, when and how to learn it, and how to capture it.

Chapter 10

Expanding to Small Groups of Agile Teams

If there isn't already a cleverly named law to describe the fact that successful teams will inevitably grow, there should be. Successful teams generate business value and create new opportunities. They get noticed and asked to deliver increasing amounts of value. Team members are added to enable more ambitious goals. The larger team becomes unwieldy and starts to struggle in ways that the smaller team did not. The inevitable split into two smaller teams creates more success but adds a whole different set of problems. When programs incorporate multiple teams, teams will need to start developing processes for coordinating their overall delivery work.

How Many Product Owners Should There Be?

As programs grow in size to the point where they have more than one team or a small cluster of teams, it is critical to consider whether they can still be handled by a single Product Owner. The role of Product Owner happens to be one of the roles in Agile that doesn't scale very well. Even a good, experienced, engaged Product Owner with no other commitments (clearly a fictional character) can handle two Agile teams at the very most. Scrum Masters scale a little better, but a full-time Scrum Master can still only handle three teams simultaneously. Sometimes, growing programs in this situation will ask other team members to do double duty as Scrum Master. Avoid this anti-pattern if possible, as it creates conflicts of interest.

DOI: 10.4324/9781003188520-14

Updating Team Topology

There are a variety of new activities and responsibilities that go along with coordinating distributed design and research in an Agile environment. New people are often brought in specifically to manage or conduct team coordination activities, particularly when teams are struggling to handle the extra HCD responsibilities and maintain their velocity or when consensus gets harder to reach.

Design or Creative Lead—This person is responsible for defining design standards and ensuring they are followed to the degree required. They are also responsible for ensuring that tools and templates are maintained and evaluating design work at a program level to certify that the quality of design is appropriate.

Research Coordinator—This person is responsible for the maintenance of any materials described in the research ops section, ensuring that research is planned in such a way that there is enough time for it to be designed and conducted with added time for teams to ingest those insights within their delivery cycle.

Recruitment Coordinator—Because recruiting is one of the "heaviest" parts of the research process, it is very common to have someone handle all the details and activities of recruitment for the necessary research.

Sometimes, the first two roles are combined into something that sounds more like a "UX Architect" or another generalized design leadership role that has tasks above the individual contributor layer. And while a new role doesn't *necessarily* mean a new person to conduct that activity, it does require that time be set aside for the planning and coordination activities themselves.

Scrum of Scrums—Organically Scaling Scrum

More people means longer and less productive meetings. This is one of the first problems teams encounter when trying to scale Scrum. A common pattern to work around this issue is to scale the daily standup (technically called the "daily scrum") to a higher level "Scrum of Scrums, (shown in Figure 10.1). This daily "Scrum of Scrums" involves only one or two people from each team, specifically to keep the membership small and the meeting timebox tight. Where teams are concerned, smaller is better.

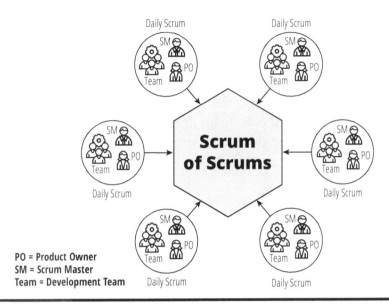

Figure 10.1   A small cluster of teams and a Scrum of Scrums.

Any impediments that cannot be removed by the team themselves or by their Scrum Master are brought to the scrum of scrums. Scrum Masters attend as do people with the best knowledge about whatever issues the teams are facing. Scrum Masters take turns facilitating these meetings, and anything learned at this meeting is then taken back to the teams immediately.

Team Alignment Activities

Intake, Problem Definition, and Communicating Design Goals

It is critical to practice the proper initiation of work on a feature level (and larger) in Human-Centered Agile. This begins with a clear problem definition with well-written epics that articulate a solution to a user need or problem. Without a team-wide shared understanding of the impact a feature should provide, teams will struggle to move past basic task management to a more Agile mindset of creating solutions that deliver the best value and can be iterated on. Put simply, good problem definition is the difference between effective Agile and simply trying to apply Agile terminology to older processes.

Teams should start feature (or epic) work with a problem definition step, which includes defining user outcomes and success metrics. This step takes place ahead of any work that the team picks up and captures the context of the work that the team is about to engage in. Incidentally, this is referred to as a problem definition rather than a *kickoff* because kickoff is often used more expansively and can mean anything from strategic consideration of whether work should be done all the way to just being a meeting that assigns a team to pick up already-defined work.

Holistic Teams, Holistic Work

Human-Centered Agile takes a *holistic* approach to teams, both to preserve team independence and flexibility in solving problems and to see that the solution is delivered and evaluated by the team that identified and understood the problem. This "whole team, whole problem, whole outcome" mindset is an essential concept.

The idea in Human-Centered Agile is that the team working on the problem has ownership from the problem definition stage through the product evaluation. Keeping one team engaged from problem definition through solution delivery maintains alignment around the purpose of the work and ensures that the team makes decisions based on intended outcomes rather than drifting toward more convenient decisions in terms of development, which may not produce intended results. It also keeps teams from slowing down due to a lack of confidence in the "right problem" and "right solution" decisions, as that team has already worked through those steps together.

Team-to-Team Handoffs

Ideally, Agile teams work on a problem from end to end, which is true in Human-Centered Agile as well. However, when scaling to a group of coordinated teams, having a single team work through features end to end becomes increasingly challenging. Looking back at the example of creating an "after-hours support capability" that was presented in Chapter 7, the team that did the initial research might recommend a chatbot to serve some customers and a standalone application that serves others. These solutions may be too much for just one team to deliver, so another team is brought in.

In Human-Centered Agile, the team being brought in is now given responsibility for the problem (after-hours support capabilities), the solution (an application), and the outcome, including determining how to best measure success. The new team could very well learn that people don't need support ("oops the discovery was wrong!") or that they don't want an app at all ("did you all even validate that this is something people want?!?"). In this context, the new team has permission to question any previous findings or decisions and can fill in missing discovery or concept validation that hasn't been completed. Put another way, one team never simply *tasks* another team with development work.

The purpose of a handoff step is to bring the newer team into the life cycle with a complete understanding of the work that has already been done so the incoming team can be confident in the decisions that have been made and the work that has already been accomplished, is in agreement with any work that has been identified, and can identify unresolved questions. This activity puts the team on the same page from the moment they are engaged and ensures that delivery decisions or any adjustments are made with the original goals and intended outcomes in mind.

What a Good Handoff Includes

The handoff should include the following items, which should have been generated in the problem definition phase of work. If there are gaps in this information, it becomes incumbent on the new team to make sure they are filled.

- The goal of effort, described in a user-centric way
- Outcome-based success criteria so any team taking on a feature for delivery understands what will be evaluated for success
- Documentation of any user insights gathered in support of the work
- Documentation of any validation efforts undertaken to this point
- Other information that provides constraints on what can be delivered, such as:
  - known technical constraints
  - known impacts (systems, processes, or in-flight work that will have to adapt to newly delivered solutions)
  - known dependencies (systems, processes, or in-flight work that the team needs as a prerequisite to delivering the solution)
  - key dates and their business drivers

Team Formation Success Factors

An often-overlooked component of team success is team formation itself and the activities that precede launch. Agile Coaches often look themselves in the mirror and ask why the team they are coaching isn't making the sort of progress they might expect. The reason is that there is prework needed to ensure the team's success that needs to be done long in advance of team launch. Without that up-front work, even the best coaching will have only a marginal effect.

During team formation, managers must carefully consider not only charter ("What value and solutions do we want this team to deliver?") and technical domain ("What mix of technology specialists do we need to deliver this value?") but also critical ways of working issues ("How will this team work together? What are their time zones? Do they speak the same language? Do we have the basic building blocks of a real team with these individuals, or would they just be a group of people who work together?").

"Forming, storming, norming, and performing"[1] is a real phenomenon, not just an academic theory. As it turns out, the performing part is a lot easier if the forming part is thoughtfully planned and executed. Questions to ask during team formation and launch are

- What product will this team be supporting?
- How does the team's product fit into the enterprise strategy?
- Does the product have a clearly defined roadmap?
- Who are the users this team will be supporting?
- Do the individuals on the team have the time to dedicate to this product, or are they allocated to another product (or perhaps several)?
- Does the team have the automation and tooling they need to be successful?

It's easy to see how overlooking these foundational questions and jumping right into team launch can be risky. Research shows that 60% of a team's success can be directly attributed to prelaunch activities and 30% can be attributed to the launch itself.[2] This means that 90% of a team's measurable

---

[1] Bruce W. Tuckman, 1965, Developmental sequence in small groups. *Psychological Bulletin* 63(6): 384–399

[2] J.R. Hackman and R. Wageman, 2005, A theory of team coaching. *Academy of Management Review* 30(2): 269

success comes from things that happen before they start their first sprint! Furthermore, their research shows that even with competent coaching poorly formed and launched teams show little improvement. For these reasons, it makes sense to spend time on success factors in team formation.

The chief success factors for incorporating HCD into Agile programs are:

Executive Support

Without an engaged and supportive Executive, even properly launched teams with the best practices cannot succeed. Ongoing support of a powerful Executive champion is necessary to ensure that the work of the teams is aligned with the enterprise strategy. Beyond that, Executives are uniquely situated to support and anchor the mindset shift that is needed for Human-Centered Agile (or any Agile, really) to succeed. Teams need to know that it really is OK for them to "fail fast." They need to work in a psychologically safe environment where they can experiment and truly question assumptions. Team members also need not be multiply allocated in order to be maximally effective. Only an Executive can ensure all these things.

Clear Expectations for Self-Management

The whole idea of Agile is for teams to manage themselves. However, before teams start work, a clear understanding of management's expectations of what the team will deliver as well as an understanding of any constraints or limitations, such as other work they will be expected to perform. Every team has boundaries, and it is important they be understood by all from the beginning.

Team Working Agreements—At the time a team is formed, they should codify their standards, expectations, and norms in the form of a "team working agreement." These documents typically spell out the team's definition of done, when and where their daily standups will be held, the norms and expectations for shared and collaborative tools (such as application life-cycle management tools), and any other information useful in managing expectations. This working agreement should be revisited periodically at retrospectives.

Daily Interactions with an Engaged Product Owner—The active, hands-on engagement from a knowledgeable Product Owner is another key success factor. Because there is no requirements document, Agile teams engage in a series of experiments and need feedback on them. They will have questions, and since the Product Owner has the ultimate responsibility to accept the team's work. Having easy access to the Product Owner means teams don't have to wait for feedback; they make faster decisions, pivot with greater ease, and deliver faster than teams that have to wait for this feedback.

A Backlog of Problems to be Solved, Not a Task List

The most successful teams are those who are given a set of goals and then left to discover the best way of achieving those themselves and having a backlog that allows them to do this is key. The more constraints the team is given, the less freedom they have to experiment and innovate. Sometimes teams will have what amounts to a requirements document (complete with painful detail about how everything is to be delivered). That's a classic example of an organization "waterfalling" a sprint.

Autonomy and Purpose

The way to get maximum productivity out of knowledge workers is to give them autonomy to innovate. Articulate the "why" and "what" then get out of their way. Let them fail, repeatedly, if necessary. Let them experiment and innovate. Most important, let them be in control of the "how." Teams who are overly constrained in their approach by management risk applying the veneer of Agile to waterfall methods.

Purpose goes hand in hand with autonomy on the hit parade of team success factors. Knowledge workers thrive on having a purpose bigger than themselves. Leadership must ensure that they share a common understanding of this purpose. For more information about how autonomy, mastery, and purpose are the keys to unlocking innovation and productivity in knowledge workers, read *Drive* by Dan Pink.[3]

Expectation of Team Stability

Agile teams tend not to be optimally productive at the outset. Bruce Tuckman identified the "developmental sequence of small groups" model of "forming, storming, norming, and performing" in 1965.[4] The idea is that

---

[3] Dan Pink, 2009, *Drive*, Riverhead Books, an Imprint of Penguin Books
[4] Bruce W. Tuckman, 1965, Developmental sequence in small groups. *Psychological Bulletin* 63(6): 384–399

teams take a while (usually 2–3 sprints) to get the hang of working with each other. Productivity typically increases after these initial "forming and storming" phases. Because it takes a while for teams to hit their stride, a good practice is to keep teams together as long as possible. This means letting teams work through any initial struggles, an investment returned by teams not having to repeatedly go through a learning curve on how to best work together.

Team Participation in HCD Activities

Writing about how drop-in teams aren't enough in *The Science and Impact of Organizational Change*, Paul Gibbons asserts, "Change expertise is too important to be left to the specialists."[5] So, too, is it when creating good user experiences. Leaving the responsibility for creating a good experience in the hands of a few "experience specialists" leaves the team in a precarious state, because a couple of voices are often outnumbered by team members prioritizing expedient development. Team members uninterested in the final experience will *always* value expedience first.

Moving Past Small Team Clusters

As programs grow in size past the point where business opportunities can be met by a small cluster of teams (more than about 50 total people), several patterns for dysfunction emerge.

Product Owners with Competing Visions

Multiple Product Owners struggle to keep their visions unified across teams. The reason that single teams have one, and only one, Product Owner is because they need one unified vision. With multiple teams and multiple Product Owners, there are multiple visions. Some Product Owners will have differing views on priorities, while others differ on the basic needs of users. Until they align around a common mission, misaligned Product Owners will struggle to produce anything of value. This is particularly likely to happen when programs grow to a number of teams, and it becomes impossible for a single person such as a Product Owner to align vision to delivery on every team.

---

[5] Paul Gibbons, 2014, *The Science of Organizational Change*, Phronesis Media

Strategy-Level Stakeholders with Competing Priorities

In addition to having Product Owners with competing visions at a product delivery level, large programs can also experience the challenge of multiple executive-level stakeholders expressing competing strategic priorities during the product delivery process. When this happens, work gets redirected regularly (sometimes toward work that is not well defined), and teams can feel that their work is undervalued. When teams cannot identify and understand the strategic value of their work, churn, and low morale build.

LESSONS FROM THE FIELD

We presented an experience report at the Agile 2021 Conference about our work bringing Human-Centered Design (HCD) into a mature SAFe® program, which identified critical steps in growing maturity instead of "throwing HCD practitioners at teams." However, beyond the structural approach to adapting teams to include HCD work, we also recommended actions designed to help manage the adjustment of incorporating a whole new practice into an existing program already running Agile at scale.

Communicate prior to the arrival of practitioners about the intended role of HCD **and keep communicating** throughout the transitional period. A lack of shared understanding about HCD is a big barrier to effective collaboration. An HCD team can speak at an all-hands meeting and also take on outreach efforts, such as "office hours," HCD Orientation and Training Workshops, and other activities designed to foster a better understanding that HCD practitioners are not engaged simply to pick fonts and colors at the end of the process.

Demonstrate support from leadership for a collaborative effort to prevent teams from reverting to previous habits. This can be done by updating timeframe expectations, when necessary, and inquiring about how teams ensure they truly understand their users' needs and the assumed risk of moving ahead without that knowledge.

In our program, we had teams that felt as though they were already delivering to a high standard because their output was good. They needed to hear from leadership that there was a problem, that there was a disconnect between the volume of code and features they were delivering and what the overall outcomes of all that delivery were for their users, who were not having success with the tools being built. As simple and obvious as it should seem, teams don't always believe that building *a lot* of stuff is not the same as building *good* stuff.

Create a team framework that allows for activities that support HCD work and is devoted to HCD process improvement, not just the HCD activities toward a specific deliverable, for specific products.

The whole report can be found at tinyurl.com/2d2dbzjw (or, alternately, at www.agilealliance.org/resources/experience-reports/human-centered-agile-building-next-generation-agile-programs-with-human-centered-design/).

Too Many Backlogs to Effectively Coordinate

Competing Product Owners usually have different ideas about best solutions and their relative priority, yielding competing backlogs. Teams will struggle without a way to coordinate their backlogs because keeping them separate results in duplicative work, product inconsistencies, or code conflicts. Furthermore, natural ups and downs of velocity can create situations where teams without a deep backlog of ready stories or with dependencies on other teams can become idle, while other teams are overtasked. Meetings that previously helped teams see and respond to each other's progress become challenging with more participants, and teams are left with no mechanism to resolve dependencies.

While teams are busy figuring out how to share a common backlog, identify and resolve dependencies between teams, and best organize themselves, other types of problems arise.

Teams Grow to Inefficient Size

Realizing these dysfunctions, teams try to solve the problem by increasing team size. This could be an attempt to keep the number of Agile teams manageable or, perhaps, just to get more production out of an already-productive team. False reasoning determines that if a 10-person team is good, a 20- or 30-person team must be better. Agile calls for small teams, 10 or fewer members, for very specific reasons. Research indicates that the optimal team size is much smaller, closer to 4.8.[6]

---

[6] Jeff Sutherhand in a personal interview with the author, November 2017

Smaller teams are more successful because they can communicate and learn better and faster than larger teams. The larger the team, the more potential lines of communication there are, leading to slower and less efficient communications with an increased probability of a message missing someone or changing, like in the children's game "telephone." Learning slows as does Agility.

Multiple Scrum Masters Need Coordination

Not to be left out of the groups whose needs have changed with the scale of the program are Scrum Masters. They struggle with a mechanism to keep them all informed about issues from other teams as well as a way for them to escalate impediments that neither they nor the team can remove themselves. Some teams have two-week sprints while others have one-week sprints. Some teams start their sprints on Wednesday while others start theirs on Monday. Some Agile teams don't use Scrum at all, using Kanban instead, an iteration-less framework without a delivery timebox but whose work still must be planned and integrated. It's chaos.

A "Hole" in Technical Leadership Becomes Apparent

Developers struggle with maintaining coding standards across teams and even about which technologies to use. It's easy to imagine a situation in which some teams would choose Java and others C#, for example. Either technology works, would solve the problem, and has its pros and cons, but there's no way for uncoordinated teams to agree on which is best for the program as a whole. Furthermore, teams at scale need to have infrastructure (automated tools, test environments, HCD research) coordinated and delivered just in time, or they will have to wait for it. In larger programs, there are also often unique security and audit requirements that must be documented and met. As programs scale, a technical void that wasn't present in single teams becomes apparent.

Where's the Boss?

Larger programs also bring higher stakes. As the stakes for the organization increase, programs garner more attention from the senior stakeholders and Executives ultimately responsible for the success of the program. Without established standards, they will likely receive differing answers to questions and find a lack of coordinated vision among teams. Upon closer inspection, they may find that teams cannot even agree on delivery schedules. In these situations, senior stakeholders need a way to get visibility into and control of what is being built by these many teams to coordinate their vision and activities.

Larger programs need a way to:

■ Scale their Agile teams into a *team of Agile teams*, integrating the total effort into larger, overarching units of user value on a longer time horizon than a two-week sprint.
■ Plan near-term and roadmap future work that has enough flexibility to allow teams to pivot when necessary.
■ Synchronize schedules to plan and define a delivery cadence that lets them learn together, as well as a mechanism to communicate new learning across the many teams.
■ Look for improvement and innovation opportunities beyond the team level, including this new team of team level.
■ Align their technical members to a common vision around technologies, architectures, and norms.
■ Manage larger programs and budgets by using robust "Enterprise resource planning" mechanisms.

Individual teams would still like to continue using Scrum and/or Kanban, but more is needed to address these gaps. Unfortunately, despite some process additions such as Scrum of Scrums, the frameworks that are successful when dealing with single teams or small clusters of teams fall short when scaling.

The solution is a framework that specifically addresses these problems while allowing individual teams the freedom and creativity needed to be successful. There are more *scaling frameworks* than there are single-team frameworks, so organizations have plenty of options. Just as frameworks like Scrum, XP, and Kanban provide ways for single teams to apply the Agile mindset, scaling frameworks allow teams of teams to apply the Agile mindset while solving the problems previously identified as well as a range of other issues that arise at scale.

Popular scaling frameworks include SAFe®, Scrum of Scrums, Scrum@ Scale, Disciplined Agile, and Large-Scale Scrum (LeSS). The SAFe framework will be used throughout this book when talking about scaling. While other scaling frameworks will not be detailed individually, the mindset and concepts described will be applicable to all. In the next chapters, these problems are mapped onto the key roles and constructs in SAFe that solve them. Then, the SAFe workflow is examined with an emphasis on how HCD practitioners can add value across the entire SAFe product development life cycle.

Why Are Scaling Frameworks Needed?

As programs scale, they start to encounter problems they didn't have (or didn't notice) when they were smaller. In brief, these are

- a way to align many teams to a common vision.
- a way to identify and manage dependencies between teams.
- a way to plan and manage key support activities that are required by all (or many) teams.
- a way to ensure the quality of delivery across a much wider set of teams and work.
- a longer timebox for teams of teams to deliver larger units of work in.
- ways to scale and coordinate the roles of the Product Owner and Scrum Master
- a way to plan budgets and resource assignments at scale.

Once programs have a dozen teams or a hundred practitioners, running a "flat" system of distributed teams becomes inadequate because it lacks the constructs needed to scale roles, align multiple teams to a common vision, manage a common backlog, and, most important, budget and do resource planning for large programs. A program that gets too big simply cannot create a unified vision and cohesive set of processes and products without additional structure.

These are exactly the problems that scaling frameworks are designed to overcome. The trick is to solve them while keeping individual teams free to create and innovate.

THE LARGEST PROGRAMS: HUMAN-CENTERED AGILE AND SAFE®

Chapter 11

An Introduction to SAFe®

There are many scaling frameworks to choose from, but the one used most frequently is the Scaled Agile Framework®, or SAFe® for short.[1] SAFe is used here as a representative approach to scaling Agile, because it's flexible, robust, widely adopted, and already incorporates values appropriate to Human-Centered Design (HCD), making its specific practices good for discussing where HCD should fit.

For instance, SAFe® explicitly calls out and values *Customer Centricity*,[2] *Design Thinking*,[3] *and Lean UX*[4] as skills and ways of thinking it encourages teams to utilize. These specific values are important for true agility and can be applied to other scaling models as well, but they are especially important for Human-Centered Agilists. SAFe and the SAFe community website also provide certified practitioners with templates, workshop slides, collaboration tools, videos, training, and discussion forums to connect with other practitioners, which may help when new to scaling Agile.

This chapter focuses on:

- Understanding how SAFe® helps determine what the right work to do is ("right problem")
- How solutions are generated and validated ("right solution"), and how that value is delivered

---

[1] SAFe® and Scaled Agile Framework® are registered trademarks of Scaled Agile, Inc. This book is not sponsored or endorsed by Scaled Agile.

[2] www.scaledagileframework.com/customer-centricity/

[3] www.scaledagileframework.com/design-thinking/

[4] www.scaledagileframework.com/lean-ux/

DOI: 10.4324/9781003188520-16

What Is SAFe®?

SAFe® is a framework for scaling Scrum and Kanban that allows multiple teams of teams (or even "teams of teams of teams") to coordinate, plan, deliver, learn, and improve together. SAFe is a knowledgebase of proven practices for scaling Agile built upon ten principles, seven competencies, four core values, and many practices designed for scaling and integrating Lean, Agile, DevOps . . . and now HCD.

Core Values—SAFe® includes four core values[5] of built-in quality, program execution, alignment, and transparency to help dictate behavior and gauge the teams' commitment to or deviation from the SAFe mindset. These values are the fundamental beliefs and guiding principles that help teams focus on delivering value for users.

Built-in quality, not just quality, is very important to understand. The idea is that the only way to go fast and succeed at scale is to ensure the absence of defects and delivery of user value as teams progress. No matter how much testing they do, teams cannot test quality into a poor solution. The only way for teams to go fast and have high quality is to ensure that quality is baked into every step of their process the first time. This means spending time on solution validation to ensure the solution is "done right." Teams who must stop working on new things to go back and remediate problems with previous "done" work will always struggle to make progress on new work, so quality has to be built into everything as they go. There's no such thing as a "hardening sprint" in SAFe where bugs are fixed. Teams can ensure they are delivering production-ready solutions by adopting a "definition of done"[6] that applies to all their stories and covers the testing, documentation, auditing, and anything else that must be done to make their product complete.

The takeaway for Human-Centered Agilists is that these four core values should guide everything happening at the team level, the scaled "team of teams" level, and the enterprise level. These core values provide teams with the mindset and justification to do the HCD work (and related learning) that are necessary to build quality in, be transparent, and execute to the highest standards. As teams think about their processes or contemplate changes or experimentation to them, they should consider how it supports these four core values. A process change that diminishes or is misaligned with any of these four values should be reconsidered.

---

[5] www.scaledagileframework.com/safe-core-values/
[6] www.scaledagileframework.com/built-in-quality/

SAFe® Principles

Like Agile, SAFe® is built on principles that successful teams will synthesize as they customize their SAFe implementation. These principles are built on the foundation of the four values and are intended to inform the team's practices. Teams often refer back to these principles in retrospectives to ensure that their practices are in line with them. These ten principles[7] are:

1. Take an economic view.
2. Apply systems thinking.
3. Assume variability and preserve options.
4. Build incrementally with fast, integrated learning cycles.
5. Base milestones on an objective evaluation of working systems.
6. Make value flow without interruptions.
7. Apply cadence and synchronize with cross-domain planning.
8. Unlock the intrinsic motivation of knowledge workers.
9. Decentralize decision-making.
10. Organize around value.

No scaling framework can be implemented as a checklist without at least some customization. Each program and organization has its own unique constraints and needs that must be addressed. The purpose of these principles is to make the four values actionable and give teams a compass to follow when making process modifications. Teams should focus on these principles over Agile practices and consider these principles the "why" of the framework.

Competencies

SAFe® has identified seven core competencies (skill areas) in which the most successful enterprises excel. Shown in Figure 11.1, SAFe describes these competencies as "the primary lens for understanding and implementing SAFe."[8] These competencies are highlighted and referenced throughout the next several chapters, as applicable. For now, teams should spend some time reviewing Figure 11.1 to see how these competencies and their component dimensions work together to respond to opportunities and consider how they are implemented (or not) in their own organizations. Pay particular attention to the components or "sub-dimensions" of each competency; these

---

[7] www.scaledagileframework.com/safe-lean-agile-principles/
[8] www.scaledagileframework.com/safe-for-lean-enterprises/

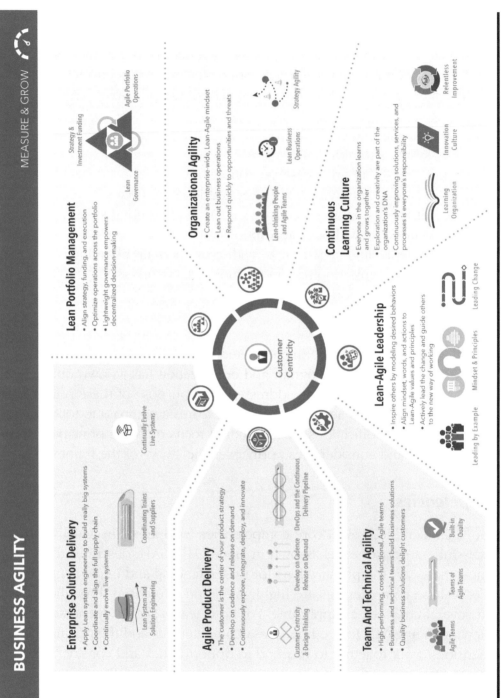

Figure 11.1   The seven SAFe® competencies and the three sub-dimensions of each.

are more granular practices that describe how organizations implement these competencies. Individuals, teams, and programs are encouraged to honestly assess their own competencies in these "sub-dimensions" and introspect about possible areas for growth.

Think of these competencies as the "how" of the framework.

Practices

SAFe® practices include new roles and new ceremonies to help teams align, coordinate, and deliver value at scale. The next several chapters detail the key practices important for HCD practitioners and will illustrate how HCD and Agile can scale together to make a more powerful way of working than when using either HCD or Agile alone.

The SAFe® website can be found at www.scaledagileframework.com. It's a rich source of information for readers interested in exploring further as every word and image on the SAFe "Big Picture" is a clickable link that will take readers to information about the topic. Similarly, footnotes in this chapter also take readers to the appropriate SAFe article. As one would expect from a group of Agilists, there is also a virtual community of practice at https://community.scaledagile.com.

The Four SAFe® Configurations

Scaling frameworks like SAFe come with considerable overhead—they incorporate new roles, events, and practices. To ensure that programs include a minimal but sufficient amount of additional overhead for their unique needs, SAFe comes in four sizes. The sizes, called configurations, can be thought of in T-shirt sizes like small, medium, large, and extra-large. As size increases, so does the number of new roles, processes, and practices. SAFe programs should use the smallest configuration possible that still meets their needs.

The fundamental concepts of incorporating HCD into a scaled process apply to all four SAFe configurations. There are two important things to understand about this: First, even "at scale," there are different needs at different sizes to keep everything aligned, and second, all the HCD work described in previous chapters can fit in at any scale. There is no reason to think that any program is "too big" to incorporate this work.

The four SAFe® configurations are:

■ Essential SAFe[9] is the smallest configuration with only the most basic constructs for smaller programs—the kind of program that may have been experiencing issues with a "flat" Agile structure. Essential SAFe adds the additional roles needed to be successful at scale, including the "Product Manager," which can be thought of as the Chief Product Owner; the "Release Train Engineer,"[10] which can be thought of as the Chief Scrum Master; a System Architect to align teams to a common technical vision; and "Business Owners" who typically have a fiduciary interest in or Executive oversight over the business. These roles are discussed in detail in Chapter 13.

■ Large Solution SAFe[11] is for programs with hundreds, or even thousands, of participants. "Large Solution" is an understatement in this context, as SAFe Large Solution programs can be unbelievably big (e.g., designing, building, and launching a telecommunications satellite). Large Solution SAFe adds even more new scaled roles and an additional level of requirements called "capabilities." These exist between features and epics and are used exclusively for integrating features produced by multiple programs. For the purposes of this book, it is sufficient for readers to know that this level of work exists in SAFe and that they might see it in their practice. It also demonstrates that SAFe can, indeed, scale as far as needed.

■ The Portfolio SAFe[12] configuration provides the constructs necessary for a robust and innovative approach to managing and budgeting a portfolio of Agile programs and aligning strategy with execution that SAFe calls "Lean Portfolio Management." This is powerful for organizations wanting to take the next step to truly "being" Agile. The tools and techniques SAFe provide in this area really set it apart from other frameworks, such as Lean Portfolio Management and participatory budgeting, an innovative mechanism for funding, and a cadence-based reevaluation of funding for Agile programs without the typical start and stops of project-based funding.[13]

■ Finally, Full SAFe[14] provides everything the model has to offer and supports the largest of large projects.

---

[9] www.scaledagileframework.com/essential-safe/
[10] www.scaledagileframework.com/release-train-engineer/
[11] www.scaledagileframework.com/large-solution-safe/
[12] www.scaledagileframework.com/portfolio-safe/
[13] www.scaledagileframework.com/lean-portfolio-management/
[14] www.scaledagileframework.com/

WHY SAFE® USES "ITERATIONS" INSTEAD OF "SPRINTS"

A quick word about nomenclature—SAFe® closely mirrors Scrum/XP nomenclature, but one of the notable divergences is in the name of the sprint. Because the goal of SAFe is "value in the shortest sustainable lead time, with the best quality and value to people and society, with high morale, safety, and customer delight,"[15] it has chosen to refer to their sprints as iterations because one can only sprint for a short time, but one can iterate indefinitely.

SAFe® also has a daily stand-up event instead of what Scrum would call the daily scrum. This is because, in SAFe, even teams doing Kanban have daily stand-ups (some SAFe teams use Kanban as a lifestyle choice). SAFe Principle 10 is "organize around value,"[16] so teams are formed to support value delivery,[17] not random work streams based on specialization, geographic location, organizational chart, contract, and so on. Finally, an Agile Release Train is a metaphor for teams of teams, and, in SAFe, these are 50–125 people who plan, iterate, and deliver value together.[18] SAFe terminology is covered "just in time" throughout the next several chapters.

For a "sneak peek," take a look at the SAFe Glossary at www.scaledagileframework.com/glossary/.

---

[15] www.scaledagileframework.com/lean-agile-mindset/
[16] www.scaledagileframework.com/oarganize-around-value/
[17] www.scaledagileframework.com/development-value-streams/
[18] www.scaledagileframework.com/agile-release-train/

Chapter 12

Updating Requirements and Processes at Scale

The SAFe® Requirements Model

Much of the terminology SAFe® uses to manage work (epics, features, and stories) will be familiar to anyone who has worked in an Agile environment before. SAFe also has designated "enabler" work, which is work designed to support the team-building features.[1] (Design and research ops discussed in Chapter 10 would be good examples of enabler work in SAFe.)

Even though the terms are familiar, it is worth taking the time to understand what they mean, specifically within the SAFe® context.

Epics

Epics[2] are the largest unit of work in SAFe® and can take multiple teams many months or longer to complete. Just like epics in a non-SAFe context, they consume significant resources and, as such, require some oversight by business owners (the senior-level manager role, see Chapter 15) and other senior leaders. When epics are first created, a Lean business case[3] is

---

[1] www.scaledagileframework.com/enablers/

[2] www.scaledagileframework.com/epic/

[3] www.scaledagileframework.com/epic/

DOI: 10.4324/9781003188520-17

generated (the keyword being Lean . . . no longer than a page or two) to help Executives understand what purpose it serves and why they should fund it and give them the basis for making a go/no-go decision on whether to pursue it. A benefit hypothesis is also generated, which helps teams evaluate the outcome of their early work to determine if their approach is sound. Both the Lean business case and benefit hypothesis are part of the minimal viable product (MVP)[4] definition.

As with any Agile MVP, the team strives to build a small, inexpensive piece of usable functionality that tests their approach and outcome so the benefit hypothesis can be evaluated and a pivot or persevere decision made. Teams frequently build multiple lightweight prototypes to get feedback and reduce cost and risk before committing to an approach to building their solution. MVP evaluation, using the Lean business case and benefit hypothesis, is an application of the Lean start-up cycle discussed in Chapter 3.

It should be considered a *success* even if the approach taken *doesn't* prove the benefit hypothesis because a minimal amount of time and money has been spent. Learning which solutions don't work early on is a win because it prevents bad investments of time and money and allows alternative methods to be tried sooner.

Features

Epics are decomposed into features,[5] which are still too big to be done by a single team in a single iteration but are purposefully small enough to be completed by one Agile Release Train (ART; team of teams, see Chapter 15) in a single planning interval, the larger timebox for ARTs to manage their work, usually 8–12 weeks. Features are prioritized and managed by the Product Manager and, like features outside the SAFe® context, deliver significant user value.

Features, like epics, have a benefit hypothesis, which helps teams focus on intended outcomes, reflect on the value being delivered, and determine whether a particular solution is really delivering as intended. Also like an

---

[4] www.scaledagileframework.com/epic/
[5] www.scaledagileframework.com/features-and-capabilities/

epic, the feature's benefit hypothesis helps teams "pivot without mercy or guilt"[6] when their results fail to prove it.

Stories

Stories[7] are the smallest unit of work in SAFe® and, just like stories outside of a SAFe context, able to be done by a single team in a single Sprint.[8] Stories have acceptance criteria that let the team know when it will be accepted by the Product Owner, but they are too small for their own benefit hypothesis. Stories are prioritized and managed by the Product Owner of the team's backlog.[9]

Enabler Work

SAFe® recognizes that not all work is user work. SAFe calls non-user work-enabler[10] work, which usually consists of infrastructure, compliance, architecture, and exploration work that must be planned and done to support user work. Of course, the part of this enabler work that is of most interest to Human-Centered Agilists is the discovery, ideation, concept and solution validation, and evaluation work that gets captured on the Research Roadmap. The idea is that this work must be planned and completed slightly in advance of the other teams so they don't have to wait for it.

In order to accommodate this type of work across the program, SAFe® has created a planning and backlog tool, called an Architectural Runway. It should be noted that HCD work is a part of the exploration enablers in this backlog. The intersection of the SAFe Architectural Runway and a Research Roadmap are discussed in Chapter 14.

The Program Backlog

The program backlog comprises the features (not stories) to be delivered by the ART and is owned by the Product Manager, who has the responsibility for prioritizing and accepting these features (just as a Product Owner

---

[6] www.scaledagileframework.com/lean-agile-mindset/

[7] www.scaledagileframework.com/story/

[8] www.scaledagileframework.com/iterations/

[9] www.scaledagileframework.com/team-backlog/

[10] www.scaledagileframework.com/enablers/

prioritizes the stories at the team level).[11] Unlike stories that comprise individual team backlogs (both inside and outside the SAFe® context), this backlog consists of much larger pieces of work that multiple teams must collaborate to compete over a much longer time.

New Planning and Delivery Timebox in SAFe®

An advantage of SAFe® is its flexibility regarding how long work takes. At a certain size, programs inevitably start considering larger work and, therefore, must operate on longer timeframes than a two-week sprint. This does not make it any less Agile. Having a deeper view of the program's backlog does not mean teams are suddenly responsible for delivering big books of exhaustive requirements covering 12 weeks' worth of work (typically, the stories in later sprints are still being written and reviewed). It just means that the epics have enough complexity that the window for coordinating effort is longer. Teams still learn and adapt as they go and have the flexibility and responsibility for planning and implementing their work. For Human-Centered Agile, it means that teams should have enough lead time to plan, conduct, and synthesize research activities in a way that informs decisions and improves the delivered product. This longer timebox helps them plan that work.

The Planning Interval (PI)

To accommodate work that is more complex and requires a longer runway, SAFe® uses a longer timebox planning interval, or PI[12]—a series of iterations for which the work is related. A planning interval is usually 8–12 weeks long (4–6 sprints) and strives to keep the entire program aligned to a common vision and the work stable for long enough periods that allow for coordinated progress yet remain short enough so teams can adjust and react to the learning happening along the way. During the PI, teams explore, plan, build, integrate, test, and deploy together, with an integrated system demo every two weeks providing regular opportunities to test hypotheses, evaluate assumptions, and pivot when necessary.

---

[11] www.scaledagileframework.com/program-and-solution-backlogs/
[12] www.scaledagileframework.com/planning-interval/

Why Is "Lean" Used So Much in SAFe®?

SAFe® describes itself as integrating "the power of Lean, Agile, and DevOps into a comprehensive operating system that helps enterprises thrive in the digital age by delivering innovative products and services faster, more predictably, and with higher quality."[13] We would, obviously, add HCD to this list.

Chapter 2 introduced the Lean start-up cycle and Lean thinking. Practitioners who spend any time at all on the SAFe® website will notice Lean is referenced frequently because it has a Lean business case,[14] Lean portfolio management,[15] a modified Lean canvas,[16] Lean-Agile leaders,[17] and so on.

Lean thinking and the Lean mindset are very similar to Agile thinking and the Agile mindset. Both are focused on high-quality, continuous improvement; eliminating waste; and solving the root causes of problems (not just their symptoms). When Lean is used in SAFe®, it means sufficient but not overly so. The Lean business case, for example, contains enough information for stakeholders to make informed decisions about whether to fund an epic, but it does not contain any unnecessary information or take 12 people a month to write it (it's a page or two long and takes about an hour to write). Spending more time than necessary is seen as a form of Lean waste (Lean places waste into several categories and focuses on eliminating them).

So, Lean isn't just another meaningless buzzword, SAFe® really does integrate Lean and Agile, like chocolate and peanut butter. Lean was around for decades before Agile and has lots of tools and thinking to help Agilists improve their processes.

---

[13] https://scaledagileframework.com/safe/
[14] www.scaledagileframework.com/epic/
[15] www.scaledagileframework.com/lean-portfolio-management/
[16] www.scaledagileframework.com/enterprise/
[17] www.scaledagileframework.com/lean-agile-leadership/

New Processes at Scale

Along with more teams, larger units of work, and a longer timebox in which to deliver comes some additional processes designed to keep teams aligned, manage dependencies, and improve the process.

Planning Interval (PI) Planning

In SAFe®, the entire ART gets together (in person, if possible) for two days at the end of each PI to identify risks and dependencies and plan their work for the next PI, a seminal (and fun!) event in SAFe known as planning interval planning (PI planning).[18] Many people new to SAFe® misunderstand PI planning and think, because it has the word *planning* in its name, that this is the only planning teams do, which is not the case. The purpose of PI planning is to ferret out risks and dependencies, not to leave with a detailed plan locked in. Note that Planning Interval used to be called Program Increment in previous versions of SAFe.

PI planning must be a structured event because there are so many people involved, and they all have to be aligned to a common strategy, vision, and architecture. Every team is asked to make sure it has clearly articulated objectives covering the duration of the PI that reflect and support the overall vision. During the PI planning process, teams can see and discuss the objectives and work of other teams and perform exercises specifically to identify dependencies and evaluate expected value from solving the problems each team is tackling.

These events usually start with Executives, Product Managers, and System Architects aligning the teams around a common vision of why, what, and how they will be building (in that order). The Executive explains the strategy, how the work to be planned is aligned with that strategy, and why it is important. The Product Manager explains the top features prioritized for the PI, what value they deliver for users, and what the benefit hypothesis and acceptance criteria are. The System Architect goes last and aligns groups on the technologies to be used, norms for technology usage, and any other technical practices necessary to keep teams aligned to a common technical vision. An Experience Architect may present experiment results or user insight gathered over the last PI, the current evaluative approach, and any

---

[18] www.scaledagileframework.com/pi-planning/

new approaches to the overall experience directions to be considered, paying special attention to pivots in strategy made as a result of this insight.

After these briefings, teams go into their own areas (usually with easel pads or, better yet, walls of easel pads) for breakout sessions, decomposing the prioritized features, identifying risks and dependencies with other teams, and developing a high-level plan for the work. The teams summarize their goals as a set of objectives written in business language that is then approved and assigned business value by the Business Owners. Teams commit to these objectives for the upcoming PI, but they will not commit to stories for each sprint in the PI, retaining the freedom to do sprint planning every two weeks while taking learning into account at each sprint. Teams present their plans so they are transparent to all and identify and review risks so the program can do a confidence vote before adjourning to ensure all teams are confident in their ability to deliver on the plan.

HCD practitioners should float from team to team, listening to and observing what is being planned for assumptions and anything else that is disconnected from the sentiment of the end user.

THE CONFIDENCE VOTE THAT CHANGED THE PROGRAM

We once facilitated a PI planning session for a large, highly technical program. At the end of the two-day session, we performed the confidence vote, which all came back as 4s and 5s (on a 5-point scale), indicating a high or very high level of confidence in the program meeting its commitment. However, one person voted 2. Rather than rushing to finish, we decided it was worth learning why this person's confidence level was so much lower than the rest of the group's.

With great trepidation, we asked him to tell the room why he had voted 2. His willingness to share would be the true test of whether we had really created an atmosphere of psychological safety. Fortunately, he *was* confident enough to identify several technical issues he felt had not been properly addressed. His points were heard, and, as they sunk in, a collective "oooh" filled the room, which prompted the group to decide to have one more breakout session to discuss these technical "gotchas."

After a mitigation plan had been put together, we held another vote, which resulted in 4s and 5s from everyone. The session concluded, and we finished satisfied with the fact that their plan was strong, and everyone's voice had been heard.

The Product Owner Sync

Maintaining alignment with the vision among the many Product Owners[19] and ensuring that the stories in each of the Product Owners' backlogs support and accomplish the features in the program are primary challenges of the new role of the Product Manager.[20] The weekly PO sync meeting[21] ensures unity of vision and alignment of teams. On technical programs, the System Architect[22] will also attend to ensure the technical vision is informed by the changing needs of the program. This is also the point where new learning—about user preferences, the technologies being used, or the competition—can be communicated from the team level to the program level. It is essential this communication be bidirectional, so opportunities are not missed. Strategy cannot be a top-down directive from Executives. It must be a conversation between Executives, Product Managers, and teams. Strategy is covered in greater detail later in this chapter in the section on the strategic portfolio review.

In SAFe,® the roles of the Product Manager and the Product Owner are separate and distinct. Product Managers work at the ART level and are responsible for features, sets of work so large that they require the entire ART up to a PI to complete. Product Owners, however, work with individual Agile teams and are responsible for stories, a much smaller unit of work that a single team can complete in one iteration. The Product Owner sync or "PO sync" meeting is held to gain visibility into the ART's progress toward achieving its objectives and align the Product Manager's vision with that of individual Product Owners (this meeting is sometimes combined with the Scrum of Scrums meeting and called an "ART sync"). Features are often broken down into stories that are spread across many teams, so it is important to have this forum to ensure alignment, especially as learning happens and plans change.

HCD practitioners and the Product Owner/Product Manager should function as natural allies, and it makes sense to add them to this already-robust SAFe® event to achieve better outcomes. HCD practitioners frequently have unique perspectives on the product that neither Product Managers nor Product Owners have and are more able to recognize "blind spots." Experience

---

[19] www.scaledagileframework.com/product-owner/
[20] www.scaledagileframework.com/product-management/
[21] www.scaledagileframework.com/planning-interval/
[22] www.scaledagileframework.com/system-architect-engineering/

Architects weigh in on what has already been validated and still represents risk, brainstorming additional discovery that could be done to mitigate it.

HCD practitioners add value at this event by identifying areas where opportunities for research may have been missed or recently arisen due to new learning. In addition, HCD practitioners are often able to detect slight variances between planned user experiences and actual user experiences, so this meeting is the perfect spot for that. Once identified and made transparent, PMs can decide how to best proceed, and HCD practitioners can make notes so they can bring this up at the retrospective.

The Scrum of Scrums

Like the Scrum of Scrums in a non-SAFe® context, members of each team get together at least once a week to discuss dependencies, blockers, and impediments in delivery. The purpose of the Scrum of Scrums[23] meeting is to coordinate their work and escalate any blockers or impediments that individual teams and Scrum Masters cannot mitigate. This is typically facilitated by the Release Train Engineer, who is usually empowered to go all the way up to executive management for help with eliminating these obstacles if necessary. These meetings are often viewed as release meetings, during which teams discuss what is needed to get functionality deployed to production. They are, as is the custom in Agile, timeboxed but often have a separate "meet after," during which concerned parties can stay and collaborate, if necessary.

The Inspect and Adapt Event

The last sprint in a PI is treated differently than all the others in SAFe®. It is called the innovation and planning iteration,[24] and no user stories are planned for this iteration. That's right, no user stories are planned. This iteration is used as:

■ An estimating buffer for overflow work
■ Extra time for teams to integrate their work
■ Time set aside for innovation (hackathons, working with users, training, etc.)
■ Time for the inspect and adapt event and for PI planning

---

[23] www.scaledagileframework.com/program-increment/
[24] www.scaledagileframework.com/innovation-and-planning-iteration/

All the teams on the Agile release train, as well as an extended set of stake-holders, get together for the inspect and adapt event.[25] This is the critical event that allows teams to base their milestones on "objective evaluation of working systems"[26] (SAFe® Principle 5) and gives teams the opportunity to make important pivot or persevere decisions based on learning and customer insight gained from the last PI. It is also a time for management to consume learning the teams have done, evaluate the work of the last PI, and ensure that this work and learning informs their strategy. In this way, strategy can evolve along with learning on a regular cadence at PI boundaries.

The inspect and adapt event begins with a demonstration of all the work from all the teams in the last PI along with any learning, spikes, or HCD insights obtained (this last part being critical for Human-Centered Agilists). After the demonstration is complete, an evaluation of the business value of the work delivered is conducted by business owners. Finally, temporary ad hoc teams are created, and a program-level retrospective called a problem-solving workshop is conducted. In this workshop, teams identify any problems in their process, determine their root causes, and brainstorm solutions. This is how the process improves at the ART level.

By this point, the shared services HCD team has done a lot of research and sentiment gathering to ensure the Product Manager and Business Owners have the information needed to plan the next PI. This is typically a time when HCD practitioners pair up with Product Managers and Product Owners to make sure they are aware of all the HCD learning that has taken place over the past PI and position that learning so it can be easily brought to bear in the next PI. This is the last chance to add anything to the Research Roadmap that was missed or needs further elaboration before the next planning interval begins.

The inspect and adapt event itself has three parts:

1. A PI system demo, which shows the completed and integrated work for feedback
2. Quantitative and qualitative measurement, which is based on the business value of the work delivered. SAFe® has a metric, called the program predictability measure, that measures the degree to which teams keep their commitments and values they deliver. To oversimplify, this

---

[25] www.scaledagileframework.com/inspect-and-adapt/
[26] www.scaledagileframework.com/base-milestones-on-objective-evaluation-of-working-systems/

metric is the business value delivered by the team (or ART) during the PI divided by the planned business value.[27]

3. The problem-solving workshop, which is an ART-level retrospective during which the members of the entire program brainstorm their biggest problems and the root causes and think of ways to improve their process.

One way to leverage HCD Practitioners' training in reading and reacting to people's responses is to ask them to do a holistic sentiment capture during the PI system demo. HCD professionals will spread out among the group watching the demo to see reactions from a wider cross section of participants, not just those who happen to be seated near them. This is a great opportunity to look for and note outliers; when everyone universally loves a feature, but one person sitting nearby has a sour look on their face. That person might know something nobody else does. The larger the audience, the more the HCD team should spread out.

Following the demo, it is also good to have the HCD team speak with any outliers and rate/compare their "local" reactions to each meaningful segment of the demo. Was the audience engaged? Skeptical? Understanding? This can be informal or formalized to a specific scale appropriate to the team and audience. The demo, itself, is a great source of questions and ideas for future research from the HCD team.

During the problem-solving workshop, HCD can help the ART agree on the problem to be solved and then dive into its root cause, identifying what is known and what needs to be learned. HCD practitioners are trained in turning observations into actions/agreements by asking several questions:

■ What problem is the team trying to solve?
■ What will have improved when it is solved?
■ How will stakeholders know it has been solved?

HCD practitioners can ensure teams focus on the cause of their problems, not just the symptoms.

---

[27] www.scaledagileframework.com/metrics/

PRO TIP FROM THE AGILE COACH: KEEP
AN IMPROVEMENT BACKLOG

Retrospective events, at the team or ART level, held at the end of each sprint or PI, give teams time to reflect on their process and consider ways to increase efficiency. The end objective is to identify the largest problem, find its root cause, and come up with one improvement story to incorporate into the next sprint, even if that only means a 1% improvement.

Even making a minor advancement gives the team traction toward their solution. Like so many things in Agile, this strategy is based on psychology. Asking a team to produce a 1% improvement story allows them to make incremental progress that can be acted on in the next sprint. If they do that every two weeks and compound their learning, like interest, they become top performers quickly.

Teams often generate many improvement ideas during these sessions but typically choose a single story they believe will have the greatest impact and then pull that into the sprint backlog for the next sprint. They generally work on one story at a time to better balance their additional workload and because it's easier to troubleshoot process problems when only a single variable changes. Improvement ideas generated but not pulled into the next sprint can go into the improvement backlog.

This improvement backlog, along with notes on done improvement stories, is an invaluable source of information for new team members and Scrum Masters, in particular, and is easy to maintain, using something as simple as a single Jira epic, with all the improvement stories laddered up to it.

Strategic Portfolio Review

The strategic portfolio review[28] meeting, typically held every three months before PI planning, is where strategy is continuously examined and evaluated given the learning the teams have done over the last PI. Here, assumptions are challenged, and teams given the opportunity to use the insight gained to prove the current strategy wrong and make modifications, as any single Agile team would at the end of their sprint.

---

[28] www.scaledagileframework.com/lean-portfolio-management/

The Experience Architect plays a key role in this, bringing new and hard-won insight into the conversation and ensuring strategy doesn't flow top-down from the C-suite without any regard for what users are thinking and feeling in the real world. The whole point of this meeting is to evaluate "right problem—right solution" and protect Executives from making strategy decisions in a vacuum. Holding these strategic reviews several weeks before PI planning is a good idea because it gives Product Managers and Business Owners time to consider what was learned in the last PI before planning and prioritizing features for the next one. It also provides them with the opportunity to task their HCD practitioners with digging deeper into areas where more insight is needed before the next planning. This ensures their strategy is up to date with the latest insight when it is time to prioritize features for the next PI.

The portfolio vision[29] is updated during this meeting as are the constituent solution visions[30] within the portfolio. This is exactly the place where strategy meets reality in a scaled environment. Questions asked here include

- "What do the users think and feel?"
- "What did we learn about our users and the market during the last PI?"
- "How should our current strategy evolve based on this learning?"
- "Given this new learning, are there any new areas of learning that we must engage in before our next PI Planning?"
- "What known unknowns can we make knowable?"
- "How do individual solutions or products have to adapt their strategy based on this learning?"

It is not uncommon for the Experience Architect to present a "wall of experiments" here, making all their work transparent. Typically, user engagement experiments are presented in "to do–doing–done" format with a special emphasis on completed experiments that result in new customer insight, ideas for new features, or learning that can disprove previous hypotheses. Stakes are also considered in this presentation, as higher stake work will usually call for a greater investment in HCD research.

Solution Architects and other technical practitioners are also present at this meeting, which often has a technology component to it. Teams with a strategy informed by fresh user insight combined with a deep understanding

---

[29] www.scaledagileframework.com/portfolio-vision/
[30] www.scaledagileframework.com/vision/

of their technical landscape always have an advantage. SAFe® has designed this meeting to be the place where teams can "engage both top-down strategic thinking with organic team-based innovations to create a synergistic 'innovation riptide' that powers a tidal wave of new products, services, and capabilities."[31] If "innovation riptide" sounds like it might be dangerous, that's the point. During this strategic review, organizations that fail to ingest new learning and insight and then use them to inform their strategy are in danger of being swept out to sea.

Portfolio Sync

If the strategic portfolio review is where strategy is reassessed and realigned, the portfolio sync meeting,[32] usually held on a monthly basis, is where progress toward meeting objectives is assessed. This meeting is much more operational than the strategic portfolio review and is usually focused on reviewing progress on implementing epics and reviewing any metrics that the teams and Product Managers have set for themselves. Here, special emphasis is placed on dependencies and impediments that individual teams or ARTs are unable to remove for themselves. Good practice is for programs to find ways to reduce or even eliminate these dependencies, not just manage them. This can involve looking at team topology and assessing if they are organized around value in the most optimal way.

Some organizations choose to skip the portfolio sync in months when the strategic portfolio review is held. This is a mistake. The two meetings often have overlapping membership, and while everyone is looking for fewer meetings to attend, these meetings have different purposes, so organizations that skip the portfolio sync miss a valuable opportunity to check the pulse of their portfolio.

It should also be noted that, sometimes, insights directly affecting strategy are socialized at these meetings. When this happens, seize the opportunity, and do not wait for the next strategic portfolio review. Take these insights directly to the stakeholders who need the insights to inform their decisions before they get stale. This is a critical component of dynamically adjusting strategy based on insight and learning quickly.

---

[31] www.scaledagileframework.com/lean-agile-mindset/
[32] www.scaledagileframework.com/lean-portfolio-management/

Happy Hour

This is where people say what they really think. (Just kidding. Sort of.)

In all seriousness, informal meetings are essential not only to accomplish the work but also for teams to build trust and bond. This doesn't just mean having unfiltered conversations about work, but also getting to talk about non-work-related topics. In settings like this, teams have an opportunity to learn about each other's interests and hobbies and get to know their teammates as people as well as co-workers. This familiarity breeds trust, and as Simon Sinek famously said, "A team is not a group of people who work together. A team is a group of people who trust each other."

Chapter 13

Scaling the Team Structure

At a small scale, single Agile teams are largely independent with few, if any, dependencies on other teams. As size and complexity grow, more practitioners and teams are needed. At a certain point, clusters of teams become unfocused and develop competing priorities and goals. In order to create alignment across a wide group of teams, SAFe® uses a concept called the Agile Release Train[1] (ART). An ART is a team of teams, usually consisting of 8–12 teams or approximately 50–125 people altogether.

ARTs Plan in a Longer Timeframe

ARTs allow a large group of people to think and cooperate for a longer timeframe than the iterations individual teams work in. Planning Intervals, which are 8–12-week collections of iterations, allow teams to plan larger work on a longer time horizon. In addition to allowing planning for larger work over longer timeframes, having this level of visibility across a whole program means that teams and leadership are aware of dependencies across efforts. Critical for HCD practitioners, this additional structure makes it considerably easier to plan and coordinate research and design work ahead of developers picking up stories for implementation.

---

[1] www.scaledagileframework.com/agile-release-train/

DOI: 10.4324/9781003188520-18

ARTs Deliver Specific Customer Value

ARTs aren't composed of random, unrelated work. Rather, they are organized around the specific value the work delivers to users. This is important because the purpose of the new roles and activities is to make sure that the epics and features, taken as a whole, support common goals and work together in a coherent vision for success. The Product Manager has the responsibility for ensuring the work of all the teams on the ART supports the ART's overarching goals, which must, in turn, support larger organizational goals. Random, unrelated work is not assigned to an ART "because they have capacity."

Updating Team Roles for Agile at Scale

Scaling Agile requires new roles to coordinate and provide strategic guidance across teams, manage prioritization and resource conflicts, and ensure all the teams on the ART work collaboratively, sharing a common product vision and technology vision.

Product Manager

A single person, not a group or committee, must have responsibility for developing and communicating the product vision.[2] That person must understand the needs of end users and the product's place in the marketplace, which will allow them to align everyone on the ART to that product vision, prioritize their features[3] to actualize that vision, and define the acceptance criteria for those features. This person must also coordinate their vision with the Product Owners[4] to ensure alignment. In SAFe®, this key role is called the Product Manager[5] and can be thought of as a Chief Product Owner.

---

[2] www.scaledagileframework.com/vision/
[3] www.scaledagileframework.com/features-and-capabilities/
[4] www.scaledagileframework.com/product-owner/
[5] www.scaledagileframework.com/product-management/

Release Train Engineer

A large collection of teams, such as the ART, needs someone (specifically an Agilist) that coordinates the many Scrum Masters, facilitates ART-level events, and coaches the ART and stakeholders in Agile practices. This "Chief Scrum Master," called the Release Train Engineer (RTE)[6] in SAFe®, does the following:

- Facilitates ART-level events and planning sessions
- Sets and communicates calendars for these events
- Tracks ART-level metrics[7]
- Ensures all Scrum Masters are aligned and impediments escalated by Scrum Masters are removed quickly
- Helps identify risks and manage dependencies
- Tracks progress on feature completion
- Ensures alignment between the Product Manager and Product Owners
- Helps identify and remove bottlenecks
- Ensures the product vision, roadmap, and program backlog are synthesized

This role's responsibilities are even bigger and harder than the description implies.

System Architect/Engineer

The next of the major new roles needed is someone to align the many teams (and even vendors) to a common architectural vision and fill the technical void that emerges at scale as described in Chapter 12. This key role is responsible for evaluating technical alternatives, creating a continuous delivery pipeline,[8] building infrastructure just in time to be consumed by development teams, and coordinating technical aspects of the solution with the Product Manager and RTE. In SAFe®, this role is called the System Architect/Engineer.[9]

---

6 www.scaledagileframework.com/release-train-engineer/
7 www.scaledagileframework.com/metrics/
8 www.scaledagileframework.com/continuous-delivery-pipeline/
9 www.scaledagileframework.com/system-architect-engineering/

Business Owner

Finally, senior stakeholders or Executives with ultimate responsibility for a solution's success are needed when scaling. SAFe® calls these people Business Owners, and they have responsibility for "governance, compliance, and ROI of a solution being developed by an ART."[10] There are typically a small number of business owners on each ART, and their engagement happens mostly at PI boundaries, although the best and most forward-thinking business owners make time to fully engage throughout PI execution. Many times, their engagement takes the form of one-on-one communication with Product Owners. Other times they might sit in on demos or, in a best-case scenario, participate with users in focus groups or other collaborative discovery and ideation.

These four roles together provide the leadership necessary to align and coordinate the ART as it elaborates the solution (the SAFe® term for the "products, services, or systems delivered to the customer"[11]) being built.

UX Architect

While not officially part of SAFe®, teams are likely to require someone to manage design and coordinate research in much the same way a System Architect/Engineer aligns technical interests. This person is responsible for setting design standards and governance, ensuring that research is properly coordinated and conducted and the overall product (or value) is cohesive with the overall experience. Without someone specifically managing experience, ARTs are likely to have "experience drift" whereby individual experiences make sense on their own but do not act in concert for a complete, holistic experience. Teams practicing SAFe are encouraged to think about how a UX Architect could benefit their programs, typically by establishing practices for design review and critique within and across teams.

Updating the Team Topology for HCD at Scale

Team composition changes when going from Agile with a few teams to Agile with many teams. The goal remains to have fully self-sufficient teams, but

---

[10] www.scaledagileframework.com/business-owners/

[11] www.scaledagileframework.com/solution/

in practice, some teams only require certain skill sets (HCD skills in particular) at specific times or intervals. Any approach to scaling Agile, particularly HCD within Agile, will eventually have to address the issue that *fully* independent teams are not always an efficient model.

Figuring out where to deploy HCD practitioners on SAFe® programs for maximum effect is critical. Ultimately, team topology and HCD practitioner deployment will depend on several factors, such as the number of practitioners on the ART, the overall volume of work, and the type of work being conducted. In a Human-Centered Agile implementation, HCD practitioners should span the life cycle of products being produced.

To do that, there should be:

■ A UX Architect coordinating efforts
■ HCD practitioners embedded on teams with the volume of work to support them
■ An HCD shared services team that can support more limited engagements and manage design and research operations activities

Embedding HCD Practitioners into Agile Teams

Some teams need enough HCD work on their own that it is worth the investment of including HDC as a direct and ongoing part of the team, while others may only need HCD support on an ad hoc basis. Embedding HCD practitioners on teams with the work to support it means they can share all the team responsibilities and participate fully in all team activities. As a result, they gain a deeper understanding of the products being built. Thus, they become more available to support day-to-day decision-making, including any adjustments during implementation that impact the end-user experience, and can provide better assurance that the experience is being delivered as intended.

Determining whether a team requires dedicated versus ad hoc HCD support involves several key decision factors:

■ How often is that team making changes to the end-user experience? Some teams do this frequently; others may have work where the end-user experience is the tip of the proverbial iceberg.
■ How big are the changes to end-user experience, and how many users will those changes affect? What are the stakes?

Scaling to a Shared Services HCD Team

In most programs, not every team requires full-time HCD support, and some (those more technical in nature) may not require it at all. A shared services team makes sense in larger programs as a way to provide flexible support for teams that don't require an embedded practitioner or that have practitioners who periodically need additional support. This shared services HCD team should operate as any other, with a Product Owner, Scrum Master, and backlog.

At a tactical level, a shared services team allows the program to pull HCD services to teams at key points, making it much easier to conduct discovery, ideation, refinement, concept validation, solution validation, and evaluation activities. In this way, a shared services team allows HCD participation to be more robust *and* more flexible within the program.

In addition to providing direct support to teams, an HCD shared services team is a natural home for design and research operations and other inter-team activities. See Figure 13.1 for a depiction of these two team topologies.

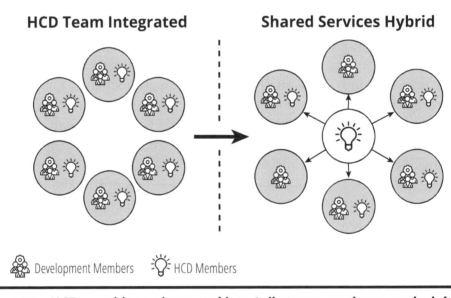

Figure 13.1   HCD practitioners integrated into Agile teams are shown on the left, and the preferred centralized "shared services" HCD team with some individual teams having their own HCD resources is shown on the right.

Strategic Planning and Support

Unless a program has already reached a fairly advanced state of maturity in incorporating HCD, teams without embedded HCD practitioners will require strategic guidance on how to conduct HCD activities within their own delivery cycle. Having a shared services team with its own Product Owner and Scrum Master who can help other teams makes it easier for programs to incorporate HCD into their work. This is because having non-HCD practitioners (Product Owners and Scrum Masters) with the ability to talk about HCD from the perspective of their own role can make an incredible difference in how well HCD is adopted into the program.

Design and Research Operations

When establishing a shared services team, the program gets a clear base of operations for all the activities that fall under both buckets rather than hoping to do ad hoc coordination among team resources to accomplish the same tasks. Additionally, and this cannot be overstated, having a centralized way to handle recruiting for research activities will save every team a tremendous amount of work.

Skills Support and Growth

HCD is often spoken about as if it were one skill when, in fact, it is a blend of many, incorporating both design and research practices. One of the subtler, yet very valuable, outcomes of having a shared services team is that embedded team members have a place to go for coaching and reflection as well as to discuss the approach to work on their team and their actual deliverables. Teams and embedded Designers can now observe considerable HCD skill growth in a way not possible with embedded and siloed Designers alone.

Chapter 14

Delivery at Scale: The SAFe® Continuous Delivery Pipeline

SAFe® uses the continuous delivery pipeline[1] as the metaphor for everything that must happen to go from an idea through ideation, delivery, and evaluation of delivered value. This chapter will focus on how HCD fits into the continuous delivery pipeline, which is seen in Figure 14.1.[2] Human-Centered Agile, when integrated to SAFe, addresses or supports all the following aspects of the continuous delivery pipeline:

- **Continuous Exploration**—The ongoing process of exploring the market and user needs and then defining a vision, a roadmap, and a set of hypotheses to address those needs.[3] Discovery, ideation, and even some refinement would happen here, but remember, this happens continuously in SAFe®. In Human-Centered Agile, continuous exploration is achieved by planning both discovery and concept validation activities that give teams actionable insight.
- **Continuous Integration**—The process of taking features from the program backlog and then developing, testing, integrating, and validating them in a staging environment where they are ready for

---

[1] www.scaledagileframework.com/continuous-delivery-pipeline/
[2] www.scaledagileframework.com/continuous-delivery-pipeline/
[3] www.scaledagileframework.com/continuous-exploration/

DOI: 10.4324/9781003188520-19

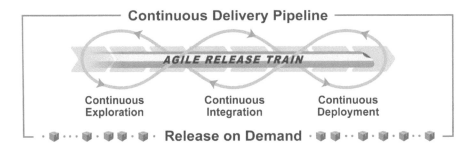

Figure 14.1   The SAFe® continuous delivery pipeline. HCD is focused most on continuous exploration, and the measure and learn activities in release on demand that can be thought of as "continuous evaluation."

deployment and release.[4] Refinement and solution validation would happen here.

- **Continuous Deployment**—The process that takes validated features and deploys them into the production environment where they're tested and ready for release, usually through an automated process.[5] As soon as a story is "done" and tested, it can be deployed to production immediately, no need to wait for the end of the sprint or for "deployment weekend."

- **Release on Demand**—SAFe® decouples release from deployment (this especially makes sense for software teams, for whom deploying is a technical decision while release is a business decision). Teams that deploy continuously put their Business Owners in charge of when the functionality will be made available to users. Sometimes it makes sense to do a "dark launch" or "pilot test." releasing new functionality only to select users in order to get feedback. Other times, the feature can be toggled on or off for everyone at the same time.[6] Interestingly, evaluation of finished work happens here (and continuously on Human-Centered Agile programs) and insight generated feeds into continuous exploration.

This section delves into the aspects of the continuous delivery pipeline that are of most interest to HCD practitioners and discusses the planning and timing of HCD activities.

---

[4] www.scaledagileframework.com/continuous-integration/
[5] www.scaledagileframework.com/continuous-deployment/
[6] www.scaledagileframework.com/release-on-demand/

Table 14.1 Activities That Take Place in the Continuous Delivery Pipeline

Continuous Delivery Pipeline Aspect	Activities within the Aspect	Human-Centered Agile Support Activities
Continuous Exploration	Hypothesize Collaborate & Research Architect Synthesize	Discovery Research Ideation (lateral thinking) Concept Validation
Continuous Integration	Develop Build Test End-to-End Stage	Refinement Solution Validation
Continuous Deployment	Deploy to Production Verify the Solution Monitor for Problems Respond & Recover	Design Ops Research Ops
Release on Demand	Release Stabilize & Operate Measure Learn	Evaluation

Continuous Exploration with HCD

Continuous exploration, shown in Figure 14.2, focuses on ensuring teams engage with users so they can innovate and gain alignment about what should be built and in what order. Going back to those concepts of "right problem" and "right solution," continuous exploration is the set of activities that are devoted to learning a user's needs, validating problems, and ideating and evaluating multiple solution paths to develop a benefit hypothesis.

SAFe® defines two activities within continuous exploration that are of particular interest to HCD practitioners: hypothesize and collaborate and research.[7] "Hypothesize" supports the winnowing down of solutions into one worthy of further evaluation, "collaborate" covers ideation, and "research" incorporates the discovery activities that support understanding of customers and stakeholders. As described earlier, this work is organized on the Research Roadmap.

It's a good practice for the practitioners and teams delivering the work downstream to perform this research so that as much of the shared

---

[7] www.scaledagileframework.com/continuous-exploration/

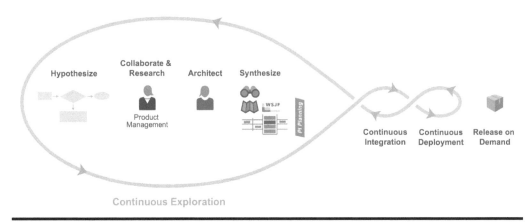

Figure 14.2   **The activities in continuous exploration are highlighted. The ones most important to HCD practitioners are hypothesize, research, and collaborate.**

understanding about the problem to be solved and user context for solving it as possible is carried through the full delivery life cycle.

The need for Continuous Exploration within SAFe® means that there needs to be established opportunities and processes for teams to do the work that generates insights about user needs and expectations, to think along multiple solution paths to a problem, and to do both concept and solution evaluation work ahead of code delivery—i.e., to "shift" some of the work "left" where learning is less costly.

Continuous Deployment and Post-Release Evaluation

Continuous deployment, shown in Figure 14.3, is what SAFe® calls the process of taking tested, validated work and deploying it to production. SAFe defines four activities as part of continuous deployment: deploy, verify, monitor, and respond.[8] In SAFe, work is moved to production (usually through automated processes) as soon as it has been tested and verified. There's no waiting because *SAFe decouples deployment from release.* Agile Release Trains (ARTs) deploy continuously while allowing Business Owners to release on demand, which can be a difficult concept to grasp at first.

Quality is built in, so the code can be *deployed* to the production environment at any time, making deployment a technical decision. Features are

---

[8] www.scaledagileframework.com/continuous-deployment/

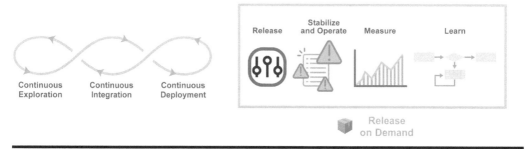

Figure 14.3 **The four activities in release on demand are highlighted. HCD teams will apply quantitative and qualitative methods to these activities.**

built with on/off toggles, so deciding when to *release* the feature becomes a business decision once it is in production. No longer must Business Owners plan for "migration weekend" a month in advance and coordinate heavily with information technology teams. In fact, most releases become so low risk that they can happen live during the day.

When SAFe® is used for software development, a domain where it shines, the full power of separating deployment from release becomes apparent. Deployment would happen continuously or, at a minimum, every two weeks. Release, however, is when Business Owners decide to make that functionality available. This makes it so teams never look back at an item and is normally accomplished through a toggling mechanism that allows business owners to turn features on and off at will. This can be done to test new features on small subsets of users to get additional feedback or release functionality when it has the maximum economic benefit.

Using this paradigm, the business can drive the release of functionality rather than having technology or migration schedules dictate the release date. Finally, this helps ARTs ensure that proper change management activities have been conducted. Commonly, such activities are overlooked, at worst, or poorly planned, at best.

HCD practitioners will have a direct interest in the way teams conduct the measure and learn activities described in release on demand. At a feature level or above, there should already be a hypothesis as to how value is being delivered and a plan for measuring it. This plan is likely to include a combination of quantitative and qualitative measurements that aid the Product Manager in understanding how well a feature is doing and investigating how to improve.

The results of both the post-release quantitative and qualitative evaluations are brought into subsequent iteration planning, backlog refinement, and PI planning. Frequently this insight will generate new exploration stories for the Research Roadmap, along with new features and stories for development.

The quantitative and qualitative evaluation activities listed in Table 17.1 are critical because a feature in the wild always performs a little differently than expected when validated in a controlled environment. The same goes for users. These activities, and the review of the insight they generate on cadence, allow ARTs to ensure that they are effectively learning from each release and improving relentlessly.[9]

Overall Solution Measurement and "Continuous Evaluation"

At the height of teams focusing on delivering and evaluating specific new features and functionality, it is essential that the program does not lose sight of assessing the experience as a whole. It is entirely possible to build a series of features that work as intended but, from a holistic experience level, start to detract by creating a feeling of "overcrowding" or eroding a product's clear sense of purpose. Solution satisfaction is rarely the sum of a solution's technical capabilities, which is important because customer satisfaction with the *overall experience* will either lead to solution adoption and loyalty or frustration and abandonment.

The product management team (Product Manager, RTE, System Architect/ Engineer, and UX Architect) should generate a plan for solution-level evaluation, which is typically more than the sum of all the feature-level evaluations. It is key that quantitative and qualitative evaluation go together because quantitative measures help teams understand the "what" (since behaviors are visible at scale) while qualitative measures, by contrast, provide a sense of how users are thinking and why they are responding as they do.

While there is no official phase for this in SAFe® (all this work can comfortably live in continuous deployment), it is worthwhile to use the concept of "continuous evaluation" to reinforce the idea that evaluation does not only happen feature by feature when new functionality is released, it is meant to cover the entire experience. In this way, HCD practitioners can imagine the continuous delivery pipeline as four infinity loops instead of three, with the fourth being continuous evaluation.

---

[9] www.scaledagileframework.com/lean-agile-mindset/

The Research Roadmap and the SAFe® Architectural Runway

Prior chapters discussed "operations" level activity that provides scaffolding for teams to do their own work. Whether technical operations provide the toolchains developers will use, the design patterns, templates, and code libraries that support consistent customer-facing products, or research recruiting support, there is a certain amount of support work required to ensure each team avoids building their own mini-organization from scratch.

To do this, SAFe® uses the concept of the previously introduced Architectural Runway, which dictates that infrastructure and HCD research be delivered to the ART "just in time" rather than as a massive "stand-up" effort that sometimes resembles an *organizational* version of the old "big design up front" model that was discarded when moving to Agile. This infrastructure work is brought into the Architectural Runway and planned normally. The difference is that it represents *organizational* value rather than specific *customer* value that gets consumed by teams.

As the ART develops features within the Architectural Runway, the Architectural Runway is consumed, only to be built up again with the next batch of enabler work. This is essentially a rolling burn-down chart of ongoing delivery from a backlog.

As with many Agile environments, SAFe® tends to regard *development* work as the key work to be tracked, so programs typically have Enterprise Architects define and prioritize enabler work at the portfolio level and System Architects/Engineers at the ART level.

SAFe® identifies four different types of Enabler work accounted for on the Architectural Runway:[10]

- Architectural enablers build the runway (networks, servers, firewalls, etc.).
- Infrastructure enablers automate the testing and deployment of the team's work (automated testing tools, build and deploy tools, monitoring tools, etc.).
- Compliance enablers manage documentation and regulatory compliance.
- Exploration enablers manage research and other activities designed to gain user insight.

---

[10] www.scaledagileframework.com/architectural-runway/

Looking at this last category, however, it's clear that some work falls outside of the technical realm and needs to be included within the nontechnical "scaffolding" concept. And it is, of course, this last category of enablers that Human-Centered Agile is most concerned with, (although it should be noted that not all exploration enablers are for HCD work—there is technical exploration as well).

In SAFe®, the Research Roadmap should be part of the Architectural Runway and organized by the experience and/or System Architects. The Research Roadmap includes the following types of activities:

■ Exploratory research, such as user interviews, contextual observation, service mapping, and related analytics needed for the upcoming iterations. In addition to work geared toward specific planned features, HCD practitioners might be engaged to do broader exploratory work, seeking unmet needs or potential opportunities (right problem).
■ Collaborative ideation activities that require coordination between stakeholders (sometimes including users) and teams to generate testable solution concepts. These are the points at which multiple solution paths may be considered.
■ Concept validation research to support proposed solution concepts generated in collaborative ideation (right solution).
■ Solution validation/usability testing of designs that are in development (done right).
■ Evaluative research to support launched or released products and inform the program or portfolio strategy (done right).

It is important to note that the HCD work described in the Research Roadmap typically has a different flavor from the technical work in the Architectural Runway. As a result, HCD practitioners must work closely with the System Architects (who own and prioritize the Architectural Runway) to ensure they have visibility into this work. Many times, the System Architects will have to be educated about HCD work and its importance to the program.

Ideally, enabler work is delivered to the Agile teams who need it "just in time" to be consumed. Sometimes this is described as "laying the tracks right in front of the train." This is important because, just like requirements, HCD insights and findings can degrade over time. While some insights are durable (such as long-term attitudes among a narrow user base), other aspects (such as behavior patterns, expectations, or unmet needs) change over time with the release of new features and experiences that reach users. As a matter of practice, many insights become outdated faster than one would think.

Additionally, the increase in scale increases the need for an insight repository. As the amount of research needed increases, it becomes more important than ever to capture it in a way that is searchable and consumable across projects.

USING THE HACKATHON TO GET INNOVATION AND INSIGHTS

Hackathons are a popular activity during the innovation and planning iteration, providing a great opportunity for developers who are not on teams with embedded HCD to work with HCD practitioners.

Hackathons can be thought of as unstructured exploration spikes. Any person on the ART can work with any other person on the ART and focus on an area of mutual interest as long as it is related to the program. The results of hackathons can be bug fixes, small utility programs, or proofs of concept for new solutions or features. The only expectation of a hackathon is that the developers show what they worked on to everyone, usually at the inspect and adapt[11] event immediately preceding PI planning.

There are two common patterns surrounding general innovation and planning iterations and hackathons, specifically. First, when paired with developers on a hackathon, the HCD practitioners learn just as much from the developers as they do from users during their research. This usually translates into powerful insights about how the solution is constructed and trade-offs the development teams make when building new functionality. The second pattern (more of an anti-pattern) is that the innovation and planning iteration is the first thing pushed to the wayside after SAFe® training. Many Product Managers think they "don't have the time" for innovation and planning. Programs that leave out this important piece miss vital opportunities for learning and collaboration.

---

[11] www.scaledagileframework.com/inspect-and-adapt/

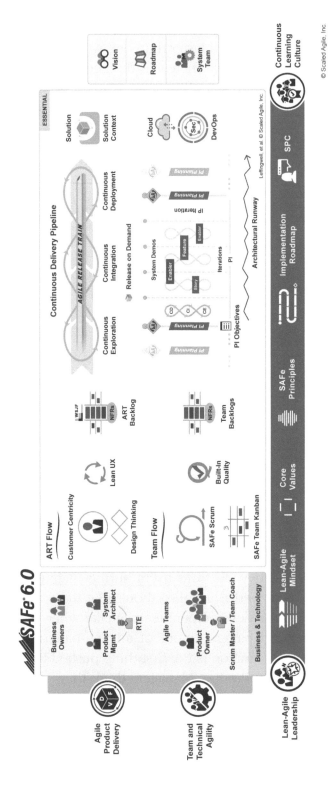

Figure 14.4 The "essential SAFe®" configuration, which contains the basic elements for programs to be successful at scale.

Figure 14.4 illustrates all the constructs discussed in this chapter synthesized into the SAFe® "big picture." It shows the "essential SAFe" or most lightweight configuration of the framework. Core competencies are shown in the circles around the perimeter (more competencies are available in larger configurations) with Lean–Agile leadership as the foundation supported by SAFe core values, SAFe principles, and the Lean–Agile mindset. The scaled roles can all be found in the column to the left, and the program and team backlog is to the right of the roles.

In Figure 14.4, the continuous delivery pipeline is shown over a visualization of two planning intervals, complete with PI planning and the inspect and adapt event ("I&A" in the figure). At the bottom is a visual depiction of the Architectural Runway, which contains the Research Roadmap. To the far right is the "spanning palette," which contains the vision, roadmap, and system team who builds some of the technical portion of the Architectural Runway. The spanning palette grows with the configuration.

MEASURING AND APPLYING HUMAN-CENTERED AGILE

Chapter 15

Measuring Solution Performance

> People don't want to buy a quarter-inch drill. They want a quarter-inch hole!
>
> **—Theodore Levitt**

In Chapter 2, design was defined as "the intentional creation of a specific experience or outcome." In the context of software delivery, there is an expected business value of providing the customer with their intended outcome (their quarter-inch hole, so to speak). It doesn't matter how efficiently teams deliver a product, if that product isn't solving a user's problem (right problem), doing it in an effective way (right solution), or created in such a way that the user can succeed throughout the experience (done right). In order to see that users are getting value out of a product, teams need a way of measuring the value delivered that reflects their attitudes toward their product.

Behavioral vs. Attitudinal Metrics

Put simply, behavioral metrics describe what users *do*, and attitudinal metrics describe how they *feel*. For the most part, behavioral metrics are also quantitative metrics—actions (clicks, time on page, registrations) gathered in large quantities. Attitudinal metrics, however, are usually qualitative metrics gathered through interviews, observation, and other techniques done on a much smaller scale. They are used for causal analyses about why people

DOI: 10.4324/9781003188520-21

behave the way they do and to create hypotheses about how new features will impact customer experience. While it often works out this way, it's not a perfect divide: There *are* quantitative attitudinal metrics (such as net promoter scores [NPSs] and surveys) that aggregate sentiment at a large scale, and researchers conducting smaller-scale qualitative research still observe and report on user behaviors.

Minimum Viable Product and True North Metrics

Every product should have a well-defined "True North" metric (or metrics) that evaluate how the team did. There may be more than one, but the number of metrics should be small and narrowly focused. Importantly, the True North metric is specific to the functionality and solution being produced. For example, if a team is working on a storefront, this could be revenue. If the team is building a newsletter subscription widget, this is sign-ups and the like. In a similar way, each epic or feature should have some *outcome-based* True North metrics for identifying whether user behavior is being impacted in a way that supports the overall product goals.

In the problem definition phase of any effort, True North metrics should be established, so when new features are delivered, it is possible to evaluate how successful the release was. This should be baked into the process at the point where the Minimum Viable Product (MVP) is formed as a hypothesis about how an effort delivers value.

Signal Metrics

Any metric meant to provide indirect information about how well a product is likely to perform is a signal metric, and there is a wide variety of signal metrics that teams may benefit from tracking.

Classic examples of signal metrics for online products are bounce rates, time on a page, time on a site, total page views, and so on. Another example is that for products with a clear path from engagement to transaction, generally there is some sort of funnel analysis to examine how far customers get into the process. If a user is dropping out at a specific point of a purchase process, that might indicate any number of possible problems with the process that merit further exploration.

Identifying Which Metrics to Track

A metrics discussion ordinarily begins with the question, "What statistics can we track?" However, all metrics are not created equal. Time and effort spent on so-called vanity metrics (the kinds of metrics that might seem valuable on a report, but do not actually inform product strategy decisions) might be wasted or prompt decisions that optimize for something counterproductive. Additionally, not all metrics-gathering efforts are going to be completely passive. There are points during an experience during which teams want to ask their end users to provide specific feedback ("rate your experience"). Instead of trying to interpret all the signals available, identifying the questions that *need* to be answered about the product or experience being created is a better approach.

These questions can be high level or granular. It is not uncommon for a team to propose a number of questions that they would love to have answered, ranging from attitudes about the product/experience as a whole to user feelings and behavior motivations during specific moments, interactions, or steps within a larger overall journey.

Once a list of questions to answer has been developed, the Agile team should hold a workshop or exercise to determine which questions can and cannot be answered and at what cost. Even decisions about how much work to put into gathering metrics are stakes-based decisions!

Simple Surveys

Simple surveys are a common tool for gathering insight directly from customers. Among Human-Centered Design (HCD) practitioners, surveys have a somewhat diminished reputation as they are a lower-fidelity method to collect feedback. When utilizing surveys, teams cannot directly observe or ask follow-up questions, so they rely on a user's self-report. Surveys may also be prone to motivation biases (only the happiest and unhappiest users provide feedback). Even with these shortcomings, surveys still have several strengths as a methodology: They are simple and relatively inexpensive to administer, can provide longitudinal information across a broad group of users, and, when created and analyzed thoughtfully, can yield valuable insights.

Net Promoter Score (NPS)

NPS attempts to boil down user sentiment into a single number by asking how likely they are to recommend the solution to a friend on a scale of 1–10. Users who rate themselves a 9 or 10 are referred to as "promoters," users rating themselves 7–8 are considered "passives," and those rating themselves 6 or under are considered "detractors." From there, a calculation is performed that subtracts the percentage of detractors from the percentage of promoters and expresses the result as an integer. Ideally, users are polled on cadence, so trends in NPSs can be seen graphically.

While popular, NPS is not without critics. The main criticism is that the score is so broad and reductive that it is of limited use. A team can tell at the highest level whether sentiment about the product is trending positively or negatively, but there isn't any indication of *why*. While this is true of the score itself, NPS can also be used to solicit comments and direct feedback, so there is at least some additional potential for a team to use it for more robust sentiment analysis. Additionally, NPS is best suited for commercial experiences. Not all experiences fit a recommend/detract model, which quickly becomes obvious for teams delivering government services or providing needs-based nonprofit giving.

Finally, when dealing with a complex experience or an experience with a longer duration and multiple touchpoints, it may also become challenging to identify whether an NPS represents the holistic experience or a specific moment/interaction. Incidentally, this critique is important for any single-score rating of a complex experience, whether an NPS or alternative, such as the Likert scale scoring system shown in Figure 15.1.

Ratings and Direct Feedback Moments

Are you finding this chapter helpful? 👍 👎
How would you rate this book? ☆☆☆☆☆ (Five stars, please!)

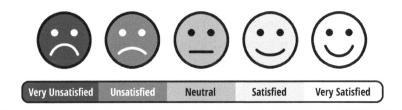

Figure 15.1 A sample Likert scale rating, which is usually presented in a 5-, 7-, or 9-point scale.

Users are regularly asked to provide in-the-moment feedback. Many times, when providing negative feedback, the user will also be prompted to offer comments to further describe any issues they encountered. Much like NPSs, these scores are most valuable when there is some sort of informative, apples-to-apples comparison (e.g., ratings scores across similar products) or a longitudinal tracking of experience (where ratings move up or down reflecting changes that have been made). These are blunt tools, and teams may find more actionable insight in specific comments than in a score. Unlike NPSs, these ratings can be more easily applied to a specific moment or experience that the team is interested in measuring.

System Usability Scale

Slightly more rigorous than NPSs are system usability scale (SUS) scores,[1] which aim to evaluate the overall usability of a system or product. The SUS uses a 10-question survey that is rated on a 5-point Likert scale and is meant to take only a minute or two for the participant to complete. This leads to results with more dimension than an NPS. The advantage of an SUS score is that the feedback received is more rigorous and specific, but the disadvantage is that it takes longer to administer and analyze. Fortunately, it's not an onerous amount of work, nor does it take a large number of participants before results are statistically significant.

The scale is calculated by asking users their agreement with 10 statements, using a 5-point Likert scale. The following are the questions on the SUS survey:[2]

1. I think that I would like to use this system frequently.
2. I found the system unnecessarily complex.
3. I thought the system was easy to use.
4. I think that I would need the support of a technical person to be able to use this system.
5. I found the various functions in this system were well integrated.
6. I thought there was too much inconsistency in this system.
7. I would imagine that most people would learn to use this system very quickly.

---

[1] www.usability.gov/how-to-and-tools/methods/system-usability-scale.html
[2] www.usability.gov/how-to-and-tools/methods/system-usability-scale.html

8. I found the system very cumbersome to use.
9. I felt very confident using the system.
10. I needed to learn a lot of things before I could get going with this system.

Custom-Built Surveys

Because surveys are so popular, it is common for teams to create their own surveys to better understand how users feel about their products. Custom-built surveys offer a tremendous advantage in that teams can build questions based on their learning goals (rather than using generic NPS-like ratings) and mix quantitative score-gathering questions with qualitative questions that seek open-ended feedback.

Surveys have a few key constraints to be aware of. For teams wishing to compare survey results across time or groups, maintaining standardized questions and employing a consistent measurement approach across surveys is important (i.e., teams use the same measurement scales and capture sentiment in the same ways as one another). Also, since surveys are highly sensitive to clarity and tone, they should follow the same content guidance that applies to any of the teams' other products. Finally, surveys are most accurate when they are completed immediately following the experience being measured (or as close to immediately as possible).

In addition to the content, it is important to consider how many questions a user is given and how long the survey will take to complete. Longer surveys typically return fewer results, and not all question types require the same amount of time to complete.[3] Teams need to balance how much they want to learn against how likely a participant is to spend additional time. Additionally, repeated survey requests can easily create "survey fatigue" among users, which further lowers response rates. Before sending surveys there should be alignment between teams and programs on how many are sent.

Other Qualitative Evaluation Methods

Interviews, contextual inquiry, and even asynchronous usability tests have all been described earlier in the context of discovery or validation. They are just as valuable in the evaluation process for products already released.

---

[3] https://verstaresearch.com/newsletters/how-to-estimate-the-length-of-a-survey/

Teams may also have planned remote sentiment analysis or digital ethnography to gain a qualitative understanding of user attitudes toward their product. Evaluative efforts require the same type of planning as in other phases of the project.

Metrics Frameworks

For teams that are struggling to identify True North and signal metrics for their solutions or features, the following frameworks might provide a good starting point. Each focuses on different aspects of their users' experience and gives a structure for thinking about which kinds of questions need to be answered when reviewing metrics.

Google HEART Framework

The Google HEART metrics framework[4] is often applied to commercial products. It seeks to measure how well a product is performing by tracking a mix of facets, like how well the product attracts and retains users, how often those users engage with the product, how well users complete their task(s), and how happy they are (see Table 15.1[5]).

It is worth recognizing that this framework, and a focus specifically on engagement, tends to work better for certain kinds of products, such as those whose business outcomes are rewarded by sustained usage. Of course, there are products, like auto insurance, that make users happy by having the *lightest* possible footprint in their lives rather than the heaviest.

Pirate Metrics

"Pirate metrics" is another term some practitioners may hear, particularly with respect to digital products. This name comes from the abbreviation AARRR, which stands for acquisition, activation, retention, referrals, and revenue. Pirate metrics are fun because teams enjoy saying "AARRR!" like

---

[4] Kerry Rodden, Hilary Hutchinson, and Xin Fu, April 2010, *Measuring the User Experience on a Large Scale: User-Centered Metrics for Web Applications*. CHI '10: Proceedings of the SIGCHI Conference on Human Factors in Computing Systems. https://dl.acm.org/doi/10.1145/1753326.1753687

[5] Emily Bonnie, *How to Use the Google HEART Framework to Measure and Improve Your App's UX*. https://clevertap.com/blog/google-heart-framework/

Table 15.1   Google HEART Metric Examples Inspired by the Work of Emily Bonnie at CleverTap

	Goal	Signal	Metric
Happiness	Is the application, solution, or product easy to use, helpful, intuitive, and fun?	Positive feedback Good reviews	NPS or SUS App/product rating Positive survey or review results
Engagement	Do users enjoy using the application and do they plan to continue using it?	Increasing app or product usage Keeps coming back Participates in online forums and/or subscribes to emails	Time spent in app or solution Mentions on social media Number of clicks within app
Adoption	Do users see value in the product or solution and are new users adopting it, preferring it over substitute solutions?	Buying the application, product, or solution. Using new features as they are developed	New subscriptions Referral subscriptions
Retention	Do users keep coming back to the application or solution?	Renewing membership or subscription Referring friends Not switching to competing solutions	Premium subscription upgrades Repeat subscriptions Number of paid users
Task Success	Are users able to complete their intended task(s) easily and efficiently?	Completed tasks Lack of errors No need for rework	Task abandonment ratio Error rate Time per task

Note: NPS = net promoter score; SUS = system usability scale.

a pirate. (Try it and see.) They are also useful in providing stakeholders of digital products a "full spectrum" set of metrics that shows them the big picture of their product's performance.

An exploration of each of these categories is in order:

■ **Acquisition**—This set of metrics captures how users get to the website. Do they come from SEO and search engines, online ads, email solicitations, public relations, and so on? Stakeholders are typically interested in the acquisition channels with the biggest impact, that is, those with the lowest-cost/highest-volume channels.

- **Activation**—This means giving the users a good first experience with the product so they will be excited about it and engaged with it. Here, teams typically measure things, like time on page, clicks from page, and any other metrics that measure the degree to which users are interacting with the product or website. Did they have a good visit? Did they purchase a premium service during their visit? How many features did they use?
- **Retention**—This set of metrics measures how often users come back to use the product or website, usually within 30 days. This metric can sometimes be improved by the right follow-up communication at the right time. Automated emails, for example, informing new users about additional features or special offers. Metrics for those emails may capture the percentage of recipients that clicked the link within to take them to the website.
- **Referrals**—This is a set of metrics around understanding which users refer other users to sign up. Products whose users are happy enough with it that they would refer friends are in a good place to incentivize this and start viral marketing campaigns.
- **Revenue**—This set of metrics helps stakeholders understand the value users derive from their product and the positions of that product that generate revenue. Typically, Product Owners will want to know how much revenue they need to break even and how much they need to make their bosses happy. Teams often measure fluctuations in revenue with respect to recently fielded or changed features.

As useful as metrics are, there is a common pattern for teams to use *too many*. As with many things in life, less is more. Don't try to oversimplify all the complexity and nuance of the product's performance into one or two narrow metrics. At the same time, avoid the temptation to use all the metrics suggested by application management tools. It is rare for a team to need to track dozens and dozens of metrics.

Objectives and Key Results

Objectives and key results (OKRs) have recently become a hot topic in Agile circles. There are even OKR certifications. OKRs fit well with Agile development because both break down large units of work into smaller units, focusing on outcomes. Objectives are larger, overarching goals or outcomes, and Agile and Human-Centered Agile, especially, are outcome-focused.

Key results are smaller outcomes that help build to the overarching goal or objective.

Sometimes, objectives are given to teams by product management or Executives. It then becomes up to the teams to determine the key results that will build to that objective. Most often, teams work with their Product Owners to determine both their objectives and the key results that build up to those objectives and then send them upstream (the bottom-up approach). Example OKRs are shown in Figure 15.2.

A deep dive into OKRs is outside the scope of this book. For those seeking to learn more about OKRs, see book recommendations in the Conclusion.

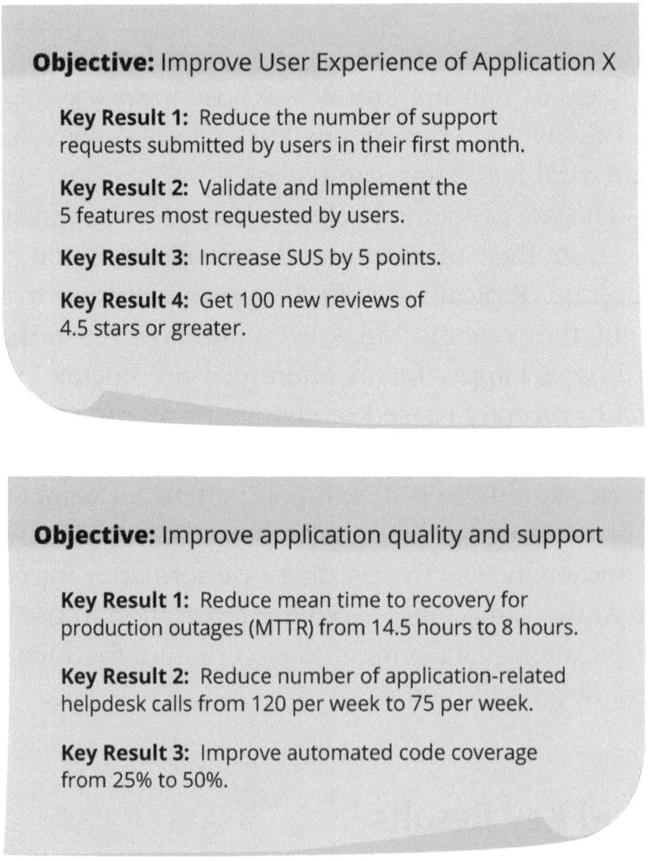

Objective: Improve User Experience of Application X

Key Result 1: Reduce the number of support requests submitted by users in their first month.

Key Result 2: Validate and Implement the 5 features most requested by users.

Key Result 3: Increase SUS by 5 points.

Key Result 4: Get 100 new reviews of 4.5 stars or greater.

Objective: Improve application quality and support

Key Result 1: Reduce mean time to recovery for production outages (MTTR) from 14.5 hours to 8 hours.

Key Result 2: Reduce number of application-related helpdesk calls from 120 per week to 75 per week.

Key Result 3: Improve automated code coverage from 25% to 50%.

Figure 15.2 Example OKRs.

Chapter 16

Human-Centered Agile Applied

As a set of steps and practices, building a Human-Centered Agile practice can sound both complex and daunting. It doesn't have to be either of those things; it is an iterative process that builds up from a few basic principles and practices.

To illustrate this, a fictitious company, DIY Fly, and their (purposefully) non-software products will be used as an example. The lawyers for our publisher have required us to say that any resemblance of the people, companies, or products in this chapter to actual people, companies, or products is unintentional. (This does have the virtue of being true.)

The People and The Idea

William always liked to build model airplanes when he was a child. He started with basic paper airplanes, then moved to balsa wood gliders before graduating to simple radio-controlled models as he got older. After college, he got a job working in marketing for a large software company, but toy airplanes remained a passion in his spare time. Over the years, he'd designed a number of increasingly complex models, being inventive with materials by using whatever he could find to reinforce his planes while still keeping them in the air—boxes, yard signs, and (most creative of all) protective plastic for electronics screens, which were thin and strong enough to protect his lightest paper models without interfering too much in flight.

DOI: 10.4324/9781003188520-22

Tom was an Air Force–trained pilot who took a job as a manager at an air freight company after his discharge. Like William, he'd spent much of his childhood working on flying model airplanes and had also carried this hobby into his adulthood. As a licensed pilot himself, Tom gravitated toward expensive and elaborate radio-controlled models with state-of-the-art electronic systems, high-tech rechargeable batteries, and other advanced features. Tom was more of a drones-with-a-camera guy but also enjoyed building and customizing his own flying models.

The two met at the local hobby store. William was there to purchase a small, rubber-band-powered propeller for his latest design, and when Tom overheard his conversation with the storekeeper, he approached and introduced himself. The two discussed William's experiments with building gliders from paper and thin plastic sheets and how he wanted to add a propeller in hopes of extending the flight time. Tom, who was heading to his local flying model club's airfield to fly his large radio-controlled model, suggested William join him, and a friendship was born.

Tom was impressed by the different "flat" designs William developed using just paper and thin plastic and wanted to learn more. Over the course of several weekends, Tom worked with William, using his knowledge of aerodynamics to help design newer models. They added an up-angle or "dihedral" to the wings, elevators on the horizontal stabilizers to extend the flight, and, eventually, a vertical stabilizer, which improved the flight even more dramatically.

Year 1

In the beginning phases, they would build various model planes and then bring family members, such as nieces and nephews, out to test flying them together. This proved to be a nice way to enjoy time outside while providing a welcome break from computer screens. Eventually, the audience expanded to their friends, which quickly came to include friends of friends. Tom and William had not intended to spend this amount of time on their hobby, but their toys were growing in popularity. As hobbyists, they used themselves and their friends for ad hoc discovery and concept validation. Before long, someone suggested Tom and William start a crowdfunded business venture, and the two agreed to explore the idea. Crowdfunding would serve as a second level of problem validation *and* concept validation.

The partners decided to build and sell an advanced version of the plastic gliders that William had been building when the two met. They sourced the raw materials pretty easily, though their small quantities made the unit cost higher than they expected (or preferred). They readily acquired paperboard boxes to package the finished product in, and the local quick print shop was more than happy to help them design labels and instruction booklets. Their big problem remained finding a way to cut the plastic. They needed an industrial die-cutting resource and finding one that could squeeze in their relatively small production runs was more difficult than anticipated. At this stage, they were still measuring success by product performance rather than by how their products impacted their customers.

After overcoming the initial starts and stops of setting up a small manufacturing operation in their "spare" time, they were pleased with how well their initial production run sold. It surprised them when small hobby shops began showing retail interest.

They wondered how they would fill their orders, concerned mostly with the procurement of all the raw materials they suddenly needed a lot more of. This enterprise had grown very quickly from an avocation to a semi-vocation. They created a legal partnership and opened a line of credit to cover expenses. They then lined up their parts suppliers and began standardizing what had previously been an ad hoc manufacturing process. Soon, they found themselves needing additional help and hired someone full-time. Then, they hired another. And another. Shortly thereafter, they had six people working for them. Despite this fact, the revenue wasn't quite enough to quit their day jobs, but it was clear that this was no longer just a hobby.

They were now a company with one product, a steady, yet small, stream of revenue, and a basic ideation and refinement process, which only involved building something they liked and testing it themselves. They gathered feedback while watching people fly their planes but based their design revisions solely on their own ideas of what counted as success, which really only included "time aloft." The way they saw it was that they were making something for themselves, which happened to have an audience, and it was great!

New Products

Excited by their initial success and the fact that they had created a small-but-vibrant cottage business, William and Tom started dreaming bigger, wondering what it would take to turn this into a "real" business so they could quit their "day" jobs and focus on this exclusively.

They developed a rudimentary product mix: a fully assembled plastic glider, a "slingshot" to launch the glider, and a fully assembled plastic airplane with a rubber-band-powered wind-up propeller. Each of these new products was an advancement on the original, informed by Tom and William's experience. And these iterations really did fly better.

All three products were launched through new Kickstarters with several hobby shops bolstering the sales, which were respectable but not as vibrant as the first round. This was not the outcome Tom and William had hoped for. It felt like they were making better products but taking a step backward.

Although they had strong sales from individual hobbyists, a new class of customer surfaced; they started getting occasional emails from teachers using these products to get their students interested in the science of flight. Sometimes they'd just get a brief "thank-you note," and sometimes they'd be asked whether the company had plans for additional products.

That was something they hadn't expected and didn't quite know how to deal with. What, exactly, did these new customers (teachers) want from their product? How were they using the planes, anyway? Could their products be improved upon for this new type of customer that they hadn't previously thought about? They knew they needed to get to know more about their customers and identify their attitudes and preferences . . . they just didn't know how.

Engaging with Users

As luck would have it for Tom and William, Tom's wife, Laurie, was an experienced user experience (UX) professional. Laurie had kept a distance from DIY Fly because she knew that engaging with her spouse's work could create marital tension and strain. However, when she saw Tom struggling with what seemed to her to be the basics of building a business, she felt it was time to step in.

Laurie told the partners they needed to spend more time learning about their customers. Sure, they knew the product, but that meant nothing if they didn't know who they were building it for, which Laurie pointed out had been for themselves, no one else. She suggested talking directly to their existing customers. They needed feedback from the people who bought and flew DIY Fly airplanes, not just from those who were already supportive of them.

At Laurie's suggestion, they first engaged in several activities designed to identify, catalog, and understand their customers. They realized they needed to better understand

- who was buying their products and, more important, why.
- whether their customers were happy with the products.
- how they could change their product mix to be more appealing.
- if their customers wanted any additional features or different product variations, they could refine and then validate those ideas.

Since they had used Kickstarter, they had a large pool of customer contact information to begin with. Despite having already sent out a satisfaction survey a month after shipping out their first round of planes, they didn't receive many substantial responses outside of a few enthusiastic replies and some complaints. They needed detailed feedback.

Recruitment

William and Tom decided to reach out to specific individuals with recruitment incentives. Excluding family and friends, they emailed invitations to an information-gathering session, offering $20 Amazon gift cards for participation. They were proud of themselves for this recruitment effort and thought they had it all figured out. As they grew, they would find out that what seemed like such a simple, easy thing was neither of those things and that it was critical to the success of their whole research effort. Years later when they were struggling to recruit teachers who spoke Spanish and who had not yet used their products with students (with a learning goal of making sure their instructions were clear), the simplicity of sending out their first invitations and gift card offers to "anyone" seemed quaint.

DIY Fly Gets off the Ground

Coordinating the interviews took longer than expected, but they managed to get a useful amount scheduled. Even after several no-shows and a handful of people providing insignificant feedback, they'd received valuable information from many participants. Tom and William noticed certain themes emerge that prompted a change in their approach to product development (and backlog refinement). They also discovered that their customers could be divided up into the following categories:

Hobbyists—The "primary" market they assumed would be their target when they started selling products commercially. These customers generally responded well to product ideas like prebuilt gliders, battery-powered planes, and templates and designs for making their own paper gliders.

Parents—The "secondary" market comprised those wanting something they could spend time doing with their kids. The product mix for this group was challenging, however, and the idea of developing more complicated products was a nonstarter.

STEM teachers—The "unexpected" market that included purchases for the purpose of teaching the basics of aerodynamics. Products appropriate for these users were design templates for paper gliders, instruction books to help teachers learn and teach the material to students, and slide decks and other instructional aides for the classroom; see Figure 16.1. During their interviews, Tom and William learned that

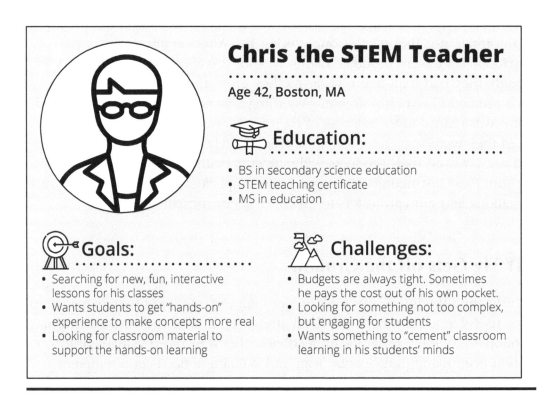

Figure 16.1   The persona of a STEM Teacher that DIY Fly developed.

this group needed to keep costs minimal, so a do-it-yourself assembly approach was desired.

Advanced hobbyists—The "more experienced" market of users, consisting of older children, young adults, and students who had already been introduced to their products and wanted to continue learning and tinkering on their own as a hobby. This group reported wanting products, such as advanced design templates incorporating more complex and nuanced aerodynamic theory, stand-alone battery-driven propellers that could be attached to any paper or plastic glider design, and simple, low-cost radio-controlled, battery-powered flying models with longer flight times.

Understanding and Capturing User Needs and Desires

As Tom and William began mapping their existing product line to the customer segments and personas they had developed, they discovered that their product mix contained glaring gaps, which left entire customer segments without a desirable solution for their needs; see Table 16.1.

Table 16.1   DIY Fly Products and Product Gaps by Customer Segment

Customer Segment	Existing Products	Product Gaps
Hobbyists	Prebuilt gliders Simple battery-powered planes	Books of templates and designs for making their own paper gliders
Advanced hobbyists	None	Radio control and directional technology Books of advanced design templates that incorporate more complex and nuanced
Parents of younger kids	Prebuilt gliders	Simpler-to-build planes More decorations and 'toy-like'
STEM teachers and students	Books of templates and designs for making their own paper gliders Simple battery-powered planes	Books that helped teachers learn and teach this material to students Slide decks and other instructional aides to help them in the classroom (e.g., aerodynamic theory in their design) Stand-alone battery-driven propellers that could be attached to any paper or plastic glider design

This matrix showed that their customers had identified needs Tom and William hadn't even thought of. Their initial concern quickly turned to excitement as they considered how to modify their current product mix to serve these currently underserved or unserved customer segments. Using sticky notes to capture ideas, they quickly developed a long list of features to fill these needs. Some of their ideas looked challenging, while others were simple adaptations of their existing products.

Tom and William also shifted away from their focus on the "moment of flight" and "time aloft," which had dominated their building to date, and began incorporating the feedback from their interview sessions to include a whole timeline and series of interactions around "flight." The other phases were:

- Exploring the product (prior to purchase)
- Anticipating the product (post-purchase)
- Unboxing (product arrival)
- Building/Assembling
- Flight
- Documenting the flight

Each of these steps held specific opportunities for improvement. Their product descriptions were thorough, but their customers had shared that the instructions for use/assembly needed improvement, suggesting that the inclusion of instructional videos and elaboration on the more difficult parts of assembly would be helpful. Tom and William were surprised by the identified "anticipation" step and were disappointed in themselves for not thinking of "documenting" as its own step. Admittedly, they weren't quite sure what to do for these, but at least they had a more complete picture of what using their product looked and felt like in the eyes of their users.

The more the partners reviewed the gathered feedback and brainstormed solutions, the more they began to understand their competitive position. Building model planes was part of the pleasure, regardless of the age or skill of the customer. People enjoyed the experience (and nostalgia) of building a plane more than just buying one. William recalled reading about how Betty Crocker learned that requiring an egg or other simple ingredient for their baking mix was more successful than making it the simplest possible product since this engaged the customers.[1]

---

[1] Despite being a famous story, the details are contested. See www.snopes.com/fact-check/something-eggstra/.

They also realized that, by providing their customers with this experience, their products were cheaper to produce. Tom and William had a sense that if they got more expensive, they might have to consider how their planes compare, as an experience, to more expensive electronics. It seemed that "prebuilts" were a riskier direction than first expected.

At this point, Tom and William set goals around their new findings. They wanted to make and test at least one new product that suited their newly identified customers and see if they could measure and improve the happiness of their existing customers from version to version. They also wanted to identify ways to improve each *step* of their customers' experience, even if only in small ways.

Laurie kept drilling into them the non-intuitive portion of having a "benefit hypothesis" for each new feature idea. This was concept validation: The strategy for doing so was to confirm the hypothesis early enough to allow for pivoting toward another approach if the early work did not prove successful. Laurie also preached to work in small batches, get feedback rapidly, and improve continuously.

DIY Fly Creates New Products

Tom and William decided an old-fashioned brainstorming session was necessary. At Laurie's suggestion, they rented a conference space to accommodate employees, customers, and potential customers so that they could have a large room with plenty of whiteboard space for ideas. They booked a whole day and had quality catered food brought in for lunch and snacks. As they held more of these meetings, they learned the immutable law of such events; that the cost of catering *good* food (not just pizza and doughnuts) was worth every penny and yielded much greater participant (and employee) engagement and happiness.

Laurie advised that they take a more modern approach than simply rolling everyone into a conference room and asking, "What ideas do you have?" Heeding her advice, they spent the first hour reviewing what was known about their customers. They talked through the personas they'd created, making sure all agreed on what the customer journey looked like. Laurie had also invited customers to phone in and share their favorite and least favorite parts of the experience of buying and flying the planes.

Next, Tom and William posted their goal: to have at least three overall new products or improvements for each persona, with an aim toward hitting as many of the "key moments" as possible. They phrased the moments as questions with specific goals, asking such things as how they could make building easier for younger kids and add more fun into "anticipation."

They started by identifying some of their inspirations—they each brought in an example of a product or experience that they really loved and explained why they loved it. Then, they did a creative exercise designed to identify aspirations: They each wrote themselves a "postcard from the future" (a congratulatory postcard from next year) about what they'd accomplished and then shared them. Finally, to get into a spirit of creative freedom, they did an exercise called "bad ideas" during which they each tried to come up with the worst new-product idea they could think of that still somehow met an objective. (This got them talking about what made ideas "good" or "bad" to begin with.) This helped them move to individual ideation work and then onto collaborative work on potential solutions for these identified goals. They discussed each other's work and then broke into different teams to analyze further.

The group quickly generated "backlogs" for each proposed product or modification. They had thought up a surprising number of "obvious" improvements, such as providing instructions in other languages and offering a sticker book for decorating the planes, allowing the younger kids to personalize even prebuilt models. Once all the ideas were captured, they took pictures for their records. There was no way to achieve everything on their list, at least not all at once, so the next day, they assigned a name to each new prominent feature or product and ranked them on their overall potential.

Tom had read about a quick, "lightweight, and actionable" way for them to separate their backlogs into four categories called the MoSCoW method—must have, should have, could have, and won't have.

The MoSCoW method[2] wasn't intended to take every variable into consideration but rather to be used as a quick heuristic for determining to build the must-haves first, the should-haves second, the could-haves third, and what not to build at all—the won't-haves (see Figure 16.2). To categorize these, they took all their proposed features and asked the entire team to vote on them. Using a technique shared by Laurie called "dot voting," they each got ten votes, symbolized by small, round adhesive labels, to allocate across the entire set of ideas and affixed their dots to the features they liked best. They could allocate multiple dots to one feature or spread them evenly, depending on their preference. Features were then roughly grouped

---

[2] Dai Clegg and Richard Barker, 1994, *Case Method Fast-Track: A RAD Approach.* Addison-Wesley. ISBN 978-0-201-62432-8

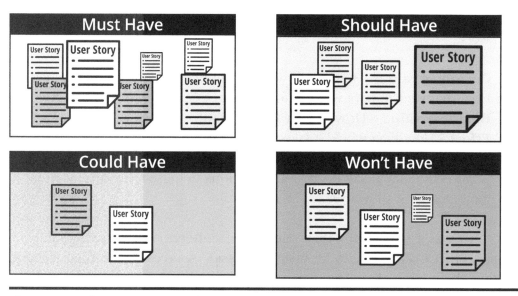

Figure 16.2 The MOScOW method of grouping the backlog into four buckets.

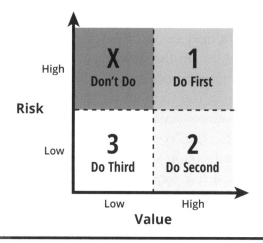

Figure 16.3 Risk vs. value in a 2 × 2 grid.

based on the number of votes, with the exception of a few stories Tom and William moved around based on their own preferences and instinct.

The MoSCoW method and dot voting had given them the momentum and focus to eliminate the items in their backlog that weren't of value, but they still needed help prioritizing the features within each category. Laurie suggested a simple matrix for balancing risk against value, as shown in Figure 16.3. Each feature in the backlog, starting with the must-have category, would be analyzed based on customer value delivered and potential risk, whether that be the risk inherent in building the product, monetary risk, or simply the risk of not doing it.

Features were discussed, one by one, and given a value for several different facets:

1. **Customer value**—How much would it improve a customer's experience? How many customers will it affect?
2. **Business value**—How does it lead to future sales or revenue?
3. **Effort**—How long would it take to make? How many people are needed?
4. **Risk**—How confident is the team in all the preceding assessments? What is the likelihood of their assumptions being wrong, and what is the outcome if they are?

Since this was a small team, they paid specific attention to features requiring skills that would have to be filled by outside sources due to their current bandwidth and skill sets. The team used the first three scores to reorganize features by priority. Instructional videos? High value, low cost, as long as they didn't mind production values that felt a little rough around the edges. Must have! An app that helps users store flight information? Between the cost of new measurement devices and the software know-how needed to build it, that idea did not get off the ground.

One team member suggested building the anticipation stage by sending out an email containing the weather forecast and park/school locations based on the shipping address several days ahead of the expected product arrival. That idea went into the "could have" category. They didn't have a software developer on staff, but it sounded like something worth checking out. Items with the highest risk required additional learning before the team could decide how to proceed.

Other high-value items with more conventional risks ("we know what to do, but it's hard to tell how long it will actually take"), along with any "low-hanging fruit," were first up for production. For the risky items, they installed reevaluation points so they did not get too far along without checking in (Was progress happening faster or slower than expected? Were there still unresolved issues that could kill the work?).

The Backlog Refinement (and Roadmapping)

The workshop was a great success. Tom and William had more ideas than they could deliver, which was both stressful and exciting. Energized, they picked the first couple of ideas off the "must have" pile, and the team got to work.

Their Schedule

Their second Kickstarter had corresponded with the holiday gift season, and it was now February—they wanted to have new products to offer by spring/summer. They hoped to shift from Kickstarter to more conventional distribution—both through large online retailers and brick-and-mortar stores. They were becoming aware of toy ordering seasons, which took place just ahead of actual buying surges (spring/summer, back to school, holiday). Presently, they planned to stick with a few distributors until they felt they had a better handle on sales and product development but still needed to meet specific dates to have shippable stock.

They decided to focus on three areas:

1. Better instructions at all levels. They needed to consider how to offer other language translations (the first thought was to pay college students for French and Spanish translations, which would cover most North American audiences). They also needed to explore creating assembly videos (and whether *those* would need to be in other languages as well) for their current and future products. This work was the "low-hanging fruit"—easily accomplished and improved the product dramatically for many users while still working with their existing line of stuff.
2. Support for STEM teachers. The list of solution ideas ranged from creating instructional materials about aerodynamics geared for middle school students to making their products more "customizable" for "experiments." This required more research, so William and Tom started working on a plan to conduct more interviews in hopes of gaining a better understanding of what would be best.
3. A version of their product "for smaller hands." Instead of doing pre-builts, they considered products that could snap together, or at least have fewer, larger pieces that could be easily assembled. Everyone agreed that, in addition to fewer/bigger pieces, including a sticker set so that the planes could be personalized was a great idea.

It became clear that the team had a lot of work to do in the next 6–12 months, and they figured more ideas would surface along the way. Each focus would occupy much of their time, and they hoped to have something for teachers before the next school year started. To help them visualize all this work, which product it was for, and which user segment it supported, Laurie introduced the concept of an "impact map," which they collaboratively developed (similar image in Figure 16.4). For more on impact mapping, visit www.ImpactMapping.org.

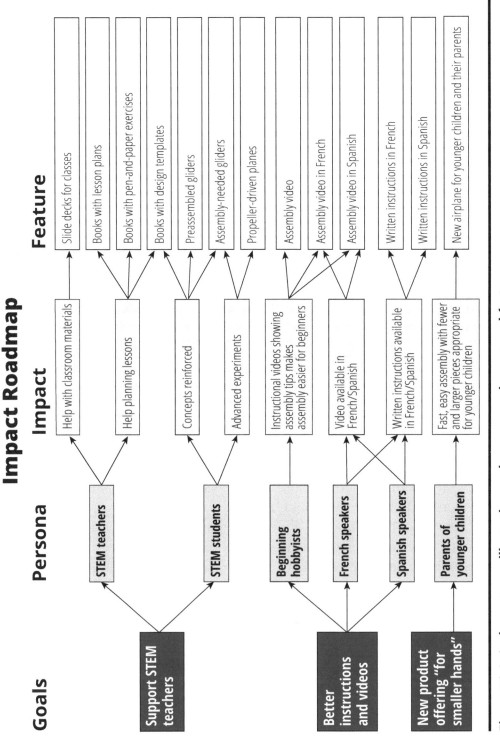

Figure 16.4 An impact map illustrating goals, personas, impact, and features.

The Workflow

At first, the new workflow was fairly simple. William and Tom had a weekly meeting with the team to review progress against the big picture. The partners remained involved in most of the work in some way, as well. Tom and William worked closely on their new "small hands" planes, which was very reminiscent of building their first products. They were able to work on most parts of this product line, including the light research on stickers, only outsourcing the sticker visual designs. They ended up selecting three sets—one would be boxed with their distributed products while the other two were offered as a bonus for online orders.

William discovered that he enjoyed shooting assembly instruction videos about as quickly as Tom discovered that he didn't. Writing the scripts was more time-consuming than expected, so William tried improvising at first, but there were too many long pauses. Even with editing, it felt awkward. Scripts resolved this issue and made the closed-captioning and foreign language translation easier. William knew that they weren't being perfect about making sure that *anyone* could use their products (yet), but he tried to include as many people as possible. He loved his planes and wanted to make sure that anyone could enjoy them, topics he later learned are usually called "accessibility" and/or "inclusivity" (more on this in *Accessibility for Everyone*, in the Recommended Reading section of the Conclusion). He learned that there are specific standards they would need to meet if they ever sold educational products directly to government clients—a distinct possibility for educational materials!

The partners began delegating many tasks, relieving their direct involvement but were still able to oversee the still-small operation. They had groups responsible for translating and reprinting the instructions, fulfilling basic orders, and managing their online product selection, email promotions, and social media outreach.

Their biggest challenge remained how to best support STEM educators with their products. They needed to spend time talking to actual teachers. Fortunately, Laurie found freelancers to assist with user research who engaged with local teachers and camp organizers. They quickly uncovered a new market that consisted of day- and week-long camps needing educational, fun activities to do with their kids.

During these interviews, they learned they could likely find camp organizers willing to pay for plane kits, as long as there was a proposed way to get a day's worth of activity out of them and the price point was low. On this note, Tom and William wondered whether they could assemble a one-week set of activities, increasing from simple to more complex activities, to support longer-duration camps.

In speaking with teachers, they learned that, despite the interest, there was little they could provide that would be part of the regular curriculum without a budget to work with. They considered building a line of cheaper educational products that could be used for after-school activities. It seemed that there was an overlap between teachers interested in running "flight clubs" and day camps.

Tom and William figured that, at the elementary and camp levels, a rudimentary overview in understanding how aerodynamics worked with the planes would more than suffice for the educational element. They also thought kids may be interested in hearing them talk about their products and thought process behind deciding what and how to build in conjunction with how aerodynamics affected their airplane designs. This, they imagined, could even be an additional instructional video offering!

DIY Fly Learns and Improves

Tom and William's initial experience engaging with customers had opened their eyes to possibilities they'd been missing. Although they had informally interacted with customers of their products previously, the insight generated through the formal focus groups and interviews surprised them. Despite the cost involved, they were both convinced of the value of continuing this engagement with their current and potential customers to uncover ideas for new or improved products.

They had hoped the email surveys would give them some insight into what was driving their customers to make their first purchase and even possibly to get ideas for future products, but as it turned out, they weren't able to learn that well enough from email surveys alone. The insight they gained through this method was valuable enough that they kept doing surveys, but they learned that they had to raise their game if they wanted to collect complete and actionable insights.

With Laurie's help, they developed a recruitment strategy for enticing a continuing stream of customers, current and potential, from each of their identified market segments: hobbyists, advanced hobbyists, parents of younger children, and STEM teachers and students. Laurie assisted them in generating a set of satisfaction metrics for their products, which they asked their focus groups and individual interview subjects to rate.

They asked their customers to:

- Fill out a Likert scale (i.e., 1–5) rating their experience for each step they had previously identified.
- Provide three descriptive adjectives, which could be analyzed to gather sentiment on the product and see what users particularly valued.
- Provide a self-report of how they used the planes (answering questions such as, "How often do you take the plane out for a flight?" "How long do you spend?" They even asked, "Do you take videos of your flights and look at them later?" to get a sense of interest in video flight recording).

Having a stable set of metrics enabled them to gauge the effectiveness of their product improvements. By conducting interviews frequently and at a regular cadence, they were able to pivot quickly when necessary. These in-person interactions with their target markets were also an evergreen source of ideas for new products. Being able to repeatedly seek feedback helped them prioritize upcoming new work, find areas to improve on what they already did well, and directly learn how well their new products did with customers. For example, they found great utility in getting help prioritizing their backlog from their customers, who curiously never prioritized it the same way Tom and William would have absent insight from users. Sometimes they would learn that a new feature was not nearly as desirable to users as improvements to existing features. This insight was like gold to them, as it enabled them to keep a constant focus on the items that provided the greatest utility to their users.

Toward the end of the year, with a few new products being worked on, Tom and William started testing prototypes of new products with their customers directly. Their first test was a fun one—they wanted to see how small hands would actually do with their "small hands" planes before committing to a manufacturing run—after all, the only way to see how kids would do with these new planes was to *see* how kids would do with these new planes. They were concerned that the heavy cardboard used for some parts would tear, but that didn't turn out to be a problem. And the stickers were a hit! (The kids got to keep the prototype planes. "They earned it!" Tom would say with a smile. The parents, of course, still received gift cards.)

Years 2–3

As time went on, DIY Fly continued growing, maintaining their focus on delivering ever-better value for their customers. After some research and reading, they found that many Lean manufacturing practices were the perfect complement to the Agile product development practices they had employed throughout their growing business. They formalized processes around improving quality, including "quality circles" where all employees, regardless of their role, were on an equal footing, had an open forum with management, and were encouraged to brainstorm solutions to the symptoms of problems as well as solutions to the root causes. They made all their work visible on a large "wall of work" and, most important, made it part of their culture to bake quality into everything they did instead of trying to achieve quality through inspection later in the process. This usually took the form of a highly detailed definition of done that included instructions, how-to videos, stickers, and everything else needed to ensure that the product was complete and ready to ship. They made extensive use of old-fashioned checklists to ensure that no steps were missed along the way, seeing no reason to change a formula that worked.

As DIY Fly grew, not only did their process improve, but so did the way they thought about their products and how they would deliver them. Tom and William realized that they had dodged a bullet (or several bullets) early on by assuming that they didn't need to be more deliberate about discovery. Armed with a newfound humility, they revisited their product life cycle with an eye toward incorporating more user insight at every phase, starting with discovery. Real discovery with real users, not friends and relatives, as had been the case early on.

At first, this took the form of simply adding more focus groups and 1:1 interviews but later grew into a whole field research component that went to model airplane clubs and parks for informal observation and sentiment gathering. At one point, their Designers ended up putting on an impromptu model airplane design workshop for a group of interested hobbyists who had gathered around. Once they saw the value of bringing outside voices into the creative process, design workshops that included a few customers became a regular element of their discovery process; their insights started to become personas, empathy maps, and journey maps—living, updated artifacts that DIY Fly employees would constantly refer back to whenever they had questions about whether they were solving the right problem. They also approached discovery with clearer learning goals in mind—would users want certain features for their planes? How much did a packaging update or a change to the product itself change their customers' sentiment at different points of their experience?

Better discovery and problem definition paid immediate dividends by focusing their thinking and ensuring they were solving the right problem. Wanting more process improvements, they doubled down on collaboration with customers and occasionally ran sessions designed to test new models that were designed to let users help them find flaws in their prioritization and product mix. It turns out, ensuring they were building the right solution was more important than they first thought, and several ideas that Tom and William thought were great (like the plane that could make a landing on water) were panned relentlessly by the user community. The more they engaged with users, the more they learned the limits of their knowledge of the market and came to rely on the only people who had perfect knowledge of what their customers wanted: their customers.

Fast on the heels of their success with discovery and ideation, they turned their attention to concept validation. Here, they formalized their learning goals and added some rigor to their existing research efforts. They found that giving some thought and reflection to what they wanted to learn and why they wanted to learn it helped them better focus the learning activities and yielded better results. The recruitment effort was front and center and, with more classes of users to engage with, got a little more complex. Different types of users were recruited for impression tests, card sorting tests, and feature ranking tasks (sometimes called "buy a feature"). This step was reinvigorated by the addition of learning goals and the critical use of something new: lightweight prototypes that could never be used in production but that were useful for gaining user sentiment. Sometimes this looked like a finished plane (that just wouldn't fly), and other times prototypes were simple paper drawings of product concepts. Tom and William were initially reluctant to spend time and money producing nonproduction prototypes. If they were going to spend money, they initially reasoned, they could sell the product and get feedback from users in the field. After a series of experiments, however, they determined that the speed of the feedback they could get from lightweight prototypes alone made them superior to gaining insight from finished production-quality work. Product quality and user satisfaction both improved dramatically as a result.

This thinking naturally led them to think differently about evaluation and improve that as well.

To assist in their proven processes, they hired a former colleague of Laurie's, Julia, to be their full-time Product Owner, a decision they only regretted not making sooner. Having a single person to focus on their backlog helped them achieve a focus they hadn't realized was lacking.

Although each one of their products was large enough to have its own backlog, the existing "common" work and dependencies between them required a dedicated person to manage it. For example, every plane that shipped had to have instructions, an online video, and advertising. Sometimes this resulted in finished products that they were unable to ship because they were waiting for the other components to be done. Visualizing these dependencies turned out to be key to managing and minimizing the bottlenecks that occasionally occurred—having a single visual reference was far more valuable than the emails and spreadsheets that they had been using previously. This took the shape of a large wall that had a sticky note for each feature and a timescale with an approximate timeframe for when the feature might be delivered. Dependencies were identified with red yarn (or a red whiteboard marker if their wall permitted its use). This way all the teams could see where their dependencies and integration points were at a glance. This was used to make Scrum of Scrums meetings faster and more efficient.

This became apparent after a few "failed" sprints that produced no value because dependencies (specifically advertising and video production) had not been coordinated, creating friction between teams that Tom and William had never noticed before, which resulted in some employee turnover. They quickly learned how expensive it was to replace someone (in terms of time, money, and opportunity cost).

Julia urged them to hire a full-time person to identify and manage the dependencies as well as coach the teams in becoming "self-managing." Tom and William failed to see the value in this and resisted the idea. Julia, referring to this necessary role as "Scrum Master," a term they had never heard before, only added to their resistance. The peculiar vocabulary of Agile and Scrum is a common barrier to adoption and not isolated to DIY Fly.

It wasn't until they attended a local Chamber of Commerce event for business owners and heard someone other than Julia use the term that they opened up to the idea. They listened to other business leaders detail their success with Agile and Scrum as well as their frustrations with nonintuitive terms, like *backlog* and *Scrum Master*, and decided to take the plunge and finally hired someone. Jeff, a Certified Scrum Master, was brought in to help them transition to both an Agile and Lean experience—Agile for Product

Development and Lean for their manufacturing operations. They got what they paid for.

From day one, Jeff and Julia's synergy was evident in the obvious improvements to their processes. They organized the still-growing staff from one large team into several distinct teams—manufacturing, marketing, and product development/improvement. The manufacturing team used Kanban to deliver the product while the marketing team used it to visualize their work and help decide, on a daily basis, the most important thing to work on. The product development/improvement team used Scrum because they found it helpful to plan their work in one-week increments (although they started with two-week sprints, they decided to experiment with a one-week sprint and stuck with it).

Jeff and Julia established twice-weekly "Scrum of Scrums" meetings to expose dependencies and risks and ensure teams always coordinated their work. This was accomplished by having one or two representatives from each team attend a short meeting to detail any dependencies with other teams. Once a dependency was identified, the other team committed to a timeline for resolution so everyone could plan better.

Each team's work remained visible on the Kanban and Scrum boards. Although the operation had grown to 23 people, this transparency provided insight into what everyone else was working on. Julia had honed incorporating user insight into a science and avoiding key assumptions and validating any substantial product changes with users then evaluating the results became part of the culture.

This mindset improved the quality and "fit" of their products several times over and helped dramatically expand sales in the STEM teacher and student market. DIY Fly became well known, available for sale in all the "big box" stores, and their user surveys indicated that they had become a trusted name in the market. However, William and Tom had no intention of resting on their laurels. Since they hadn't been taking profits out of the company, they now had a decent amount of money to reinvest, which is exactly what they did.

Years 4+

The idea to reinvest all the profits in developing new products and improving existing products turned out to be a smart move. As the number of product offerings grew (now including several different plane designs for each demographic as well as a variety of "activity kits" for younger children and additional classroom exercises for STEM teachers), their market share across all the target customer groups identified in their focus groups slowly grew. As it did it became easier to find new distribution channels and sales outlets, which added to their profitability. Their staff also grew, which brought new challenges in scaling the small clusters of teams they had during Years 2 and 3.

As their product mix grew and several products became technically more complex, they were unable to function with only their three, core manufacturing teams. They had to scale and, despite their successful use of Kanban, discovered the need for additional, specialized teams.

So, they formed a team responsible for making the electronics for their new sophisticated line of radio-controlled models and another to manage all the printing and die-cutting. Both teams shifted from Scrum to using Kanban, finding their work not stable enough, after multiple experiments, to commit to sprint goals for two weeks or even one week at a time. For example, a sprint focusing on glider assembly had to be canceled when parts were not available as expected. This frustrated the teams enormously. Using Kanban instead of Scrum gave them the flexibility to examine their work each morning and reset priorities based on that day's circumstances. They established a team to focus entirely on shipping, both in- and outbound, which used a fairly complex Kanban board to visualize their shipments from all over the world. Jeff set up a cumulative flow diagram for them, so they could visualize bottlenecks anywhere in their complex distribution system. For example, due to a fire at a large port, they had trouble getting raw materials shipped from a supplier in China. Seeing this, they were quickly able to minimize the delay to their planned production by pivoting to a secondary supplier in South America.

Another team was devoted entirely to education, which had expanded outside of serving only the high school and STEM camp market to include higher education, who found their products a valuable addition to their curriculum. This team, led by a former educator and pilot, used Scrum to manage their work. All teams used a combination of quality, flow, predictability, and solution quality metrics to ensure good output *and* good outcomes. Team metrics were reviewed at the end of each sprint, which included the number of stories and story points completed and a committed-to-done ratio that teams called their "say-do." They grouped their quality metrics around returns based on defects and those based on customers having unmet expectations. These metrics were all inputs to the team's retrospective and strictly used as tools to help teams improve; they were never weaponized or used in performance reviews.

William and Tom stayed updated on their growing enterprise by tracking epics. Jeff managed the work in a similar fashion to their methods by making it visible, limiting the amount of work in progress, conducting small experiments, and making future decisions based on the results of those experiments. Sometimes, William and Tom needed Jeff to intervene and help them focus on finishing one thing before starting another, which Jeff referred to as needing to "stop starting and start finishing."

For example, they were developing a new activity kit for younger children while also working on a complex design for a battery-powered radio-controlled plane, making little progress on either one. After heeding Jeff's advice, they quickly understood that they could get more done by limiting their efforts to one objective, even if that seemed counterintuitive. So, they put the complex task aside to focus on the product for the younger market and waited until that was completed before restarting work on their new radio-controlled product.

Every quarter, all the teams would still gather for a big two-day planning session. Everyone looked forward to the opportunity to interact with their peers on other teams as well as the catering William and Tom splurged on, which included them picking up the tab for happy hour (an important success factor). These planning sessions were critical in maintaining team coordination, minimizing dependencies, and managing risks they weren't able to mitigate.

As their staff grew, William and Tom went on to hire a Chief of Manufacturing and promote Julia to their Chief Product Owner, with three other Product Owners under her. This new management layer was needed to coordinate the activities of the many teams and multiple products being produced. Julia now ran a Product Owner sync with all the teams to ensure alignment around a vision, and that strategy continually evolved based on learning and customer insight. Jeff ran the companion meeting, the Scrum of Scrums, to ensure impediments were resolved quickly and dependencies managed before becoming bottlenecks. They even hired an electronics engineer to align everyone with a common technical vision, which became increasingly important as the technical complexity of their products grew. This group made up the core of the management team.

No matter what, their teams all met individually for 15 minutes daily to plan their work for that day. Over the years, some teams had tried variations of this daily meeting, reducing the frequency or required attendees, only to revert to the original process because daily planning and synchronization are essential to the ability to coordinate and pivot, when necessary.

As William and Tom's business grew, they found themselves feeling removed from the day-to-day workings. The passion for making things was still there, but the product lines had taken on lives of their own and been left in capable hands. This company was their baby, and, although they weren't as hands-on and could consider selling, they weren't ready to trust their products, people, or processes to another company. Instead, they decided to look for opportunities to build on their experience while offering new challenges.

In an echo of the past, they gathered a few of their most trusted employees and conducted a workshop. They returned to the same conference space room where they had first gathered to brainstorm product ideas and even had it catered by the same company (in a nod to nostalgia). This time, the goal was to identify how they might expand instead of figuring out how to turn a couple of products into a few more.

Every idea went up on the walls: drones, boats, submersibles, more advanced avionics, elaborate kites, rocketry . . . there were even a few completely left-field ideas, like creating physics tutoring services. From each of these ideas, they created a canvas of what they would need to learn or know to determine whether to go forward. They also decided to come back and revisit their mission: was it primarily hobby education or could it encompass other industries? How important was the "Fly" in DIY Fly?

In the end, Tom and William decided that it was their love of model airplanes that brought them into the business, yet they'd become driven by the educational experiences that they created. They ruled out pursuing noneducational products and, after some research and discovery work around what potential customers might use, also ruled out drones (the space was way too crowded) and rocketry (too dangerous). They settled on boats, submersibles, and a commitment to finding other "outdoor adventures in a box"—a mission that came with a name change to "DIY Launch." Armed with a clear mission, a basket of new ideas, and an approach they trusted, the future path was uncertain, but they knew it wouldn't be boring.

Conclusion

The challenges in bringing Agile and Human-Centered Design are evident to anyone who has tried to get the two working together. For it to work, teams need a healthy understanding of what it actually means to do design and research well, as well as a team (or program) that is interested in actually doing it. A structure that allows for all the tactical work that must happen before developers put "hands on keys" and the strategic value of learning to be included in decision-making is also needed.

When done right, the harmonious goal of learning what a team needs to know in order to be successful in the fastest and cheapest way possible is what makes this work. And the rewards, in terms of costly production and averted risks, are considerable.

Change is difficult. "Culture eats strategy for breakfast." Getting from Agile to Human-Centered Agile requires a mind shift, not just a bunch of meetings and tasks:

- "Is this the right problem? How do we know?"
- "Have we validated that this is the right solution? What others have we considered?"
- "What are the stakes of our decisions? Have we done enough to make sure we are spending our time and money wisely?"
- "How will we know when we've created a good experience?"

When these questions become routine, the practices of change—all the tactics described in the book—get easier and easier to apply. And, as always, Agile is as much a process-building tool as it is a product-building tool. An environment that provides safety for teammates asking questions, allows for experimentation, and, perhaps most importantly, takes the

DOI: 10.4324/9781003188520-23

time to retrospect and adapt can find success in implementing Human-Centered Agile.

Recommended Reading

For those wishing to dive deeper into some of the ideas and concepts presented throughout this book, the following list of suggested reading should help practitioners apply these ideas to their work more effectively.

Book Recommendations from the Agile Coach

Essential Scrum by **Ken Rubin**—This is a comprehensive deep dive into all aspects of Scrum. For those interested in an in-depth understanding of Scrum (and a fine reference book), this is the only book needed on the subject. Ken Rubin has even developed a visual lexicon to describe Scrum events and artifacts. This book is thorough and highly recommended.

Scrum: The Art of Doing Twice the Work in Half the Time by **Jeff Sutherland and J.J. Sutherland**—This is a very light read that is better at acquainting readers with the broad strokes of the Agile mindset than it is with the actual mechanics of Scrum. It is invaluable, nonetheless.

User Stories Applied by **Mike Cohn**—User stories are the area where Agile teams struggle the most. This is the definitive book on the subject by one of the most respected authors in the field.

Agile Estimating and Planning by **Mike Cohn**—An outstanding book for Product Owners, Product Managers, or anyone else who finds themselves accountable for schedules on an Agile project.

Innovation Games: Creating Breakthrough Products Through Collaborative Play by **Luke Hohmann**—This is for practitioners, especially Agilists, who are having difficulty engaging with users. The book, written by a recognized Agile expert, is filled with exercises that help teams understand their users' true needs.

Kanban by **David J. Anderson**—Kanban is an underutilized, iteration-less Agile framework better suited to many teams than Scrum. This book will equip practitioners to use Kanban to do more than visualize work. It is highly recommended.

***SAFe® Distilled* by Richard Knaster and Dean Leffingwell**—This is an excellent introduction to SAFe, with many descriptive, full-color illustrations, and is highly recommended for practitioners new to SAFe. Care should be taken to get the most recent version of this book, as the SAFe model is updated frequently.

SAFe® Training—Practitioners seeking to implement SAFe are strongly encouraged to take instructor-led training (either in person or virtually). There are no less than 12 different role-based SAFe certifications to choose from. The list and a calendar of classes can be found at this URL: https://scaledagile.com/safe-certification/. For more information visit: www.scaledagileframework.com/.

***Team Topologies: Organizing Business and Technology Teams for Fast Flow* by Matthew Skelton and Manuel Pais**—For those seeking a deep dive into how to form teams for the optimal flow of value, this is the book. It is not light reading and goes into considerable detail.

***Project to Product: How to Survive and Thrive in the Age of Digital Disruption* by Mik Kirsten**—Practitioners seeking to take their Agile knowledge to the next level will benefit from this book and the "flow framework" that it introduces.

***Continuous Discovery Habits: Discover Products That Create Customer Value and Business Value* by Theresa Torres**—Agile teams seeking to get better at engaging with users, building an insight repository, and using this data to make their products better are encouraged to read this book.

***When Will It Be Done: Lean-Agile Forecasting to Answer Your Customers' Most Important Question* by Daniel S. Vacanti**—This trailblazing book has changed many minds about the effectiveness of estimating with story points and has helped many teams make the shift to statistical forecasting using historical data. For those struggling with estimates, this book is must-read.

***Coaching Agile Teams: A Companion for Scrum Masters, Agile Coaches, and Project Managers in Transition* by Lyssa Adkins**—This is the gold standard in Agile coaching texts.

***Drive* by Dan Pink**—This book is less about Agile and more about creating environments that motivate knowledge workers and nurture creativity. It is highly recommended.

Book Recommendations from the Designer

Radical Focus: Achieving Your Most Important Goals with Objectives and Key Results (Empowered Teams) **by Christina Wodtke**—A fictionalized account of a team applying OKRs, this book is easy to read, and grounds the OKR approach in relatable practice.

Communicating Design **by Dan Brown**—A much deeper dive into design deliverables and how to create and present them for effective communication at any stage of the design process.

Just Enough Research **by Erika Hall**—A terrific primer on a delivery-minded approach to trusted research methods that can be implemented right away, no matter what size team or budget being worked with.

The Design of Everyday Things **by Donald Norman**—One of the earliest and still most entertaining texts about how design creates successful and unsuccessful experiences. He has also written two excellent follow-up books: *The Design of Future Things* and *Emotional Design: Why We Love (or Hate) Everyday Things*.

Don't Make Me Think **by Steve Krug**—An approachable (and even fun!) introduction to key concepts of usability and intuitive information design.

Designing Connected Content **by Mike Atherton and Carrie Hane**—Content is design. Content is usability. Content is experience. This book is an end-to-end process for building a structured content framework.

The User Experience Team of One: A Research and Design Survival Guide **by Leah Buley**—A practical guide for HCD practitioners, and an excellent survey for Agilists and Product Owners of what it takes for an individual to work as the only practitioner on a team.

Outcomes Over Output: Why Customer Behavior Is the Key Metric for Business Success **by Jeff Seiden**—A concise yet powerful book on how to shift in thinking from the endless delivery of features and functionality to the delivery of actual, measurable user value.

How Music Works **by David Byrne**—Not a "professional book" or a book about HCD, David Byrne nonetheless writes a fascinating account of how every aspect of the creation of music—from the type of performance environment the music will be performed into the incentive structure for creating it—becomes part of the listener and audience experience.

***Lean UX: Designing Great Products with Agile Teams* by Jeff Gothelf**—A valuable book for understanding how UX can fit into strategic decision-making and a practical approach for getting started with strategic experimentation.

***Accessibility for Everyone* by Laura Kalbag**—A practical approach to ensuring that designs and products can be successful for as many people as possible.

Need More Help? Just Want to Say Hi?

For those struggling with implementing the ideas in this book or wanting to share the results of their work, reach out to the authors at the following email addresses:

Joe@HumanCenteredAgile.com
Brad@HumanCenteredAgile.com
You can also connect with us on LinkedIn:
www.linkedin.com/in/joemontalbano/
www.linkedin.com/in/brad-lehman-hca/

Index

Note: numbers in **bold** indicate a table. Numbers in *italics* indicate a figure on the corresponding page.